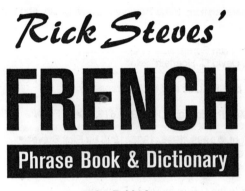

Rick Steves'

FRENCH

Phrase Book & Dictionary

4th Edition

John Muir Publications
Santa Fe, New Mexico

ii

Thanks to the team of people at *Europe Through the Back Door* who helped make this book possible: Dave Hoerlein, Mary Carlson, Mary Romano, Danna Brumley, and . . .

French translation: Scott Bernhard, Steve Smith, and Paul Desloover
Phonetics: Risa Laib
Layout: Rich Sorensen and Colleen Murphy
Maps: David C. Hoerlein

Edited by Risa Laib and Rich Sorensen

John Muir Publications, P.O. Box 613, Santa Fe, NM 87504

Printed in the U.S.A. by Banta Company
Fourth edition. First printing March 1999

ISBN 1-56261-476-2

Cover photos: Arc d'Triomphe, Paris, France;
               © Jeff Greenberg/Unicorn Stock Photos
               Foreground photo: Rick Steves

Distributed to the book trade by
Publishers Group West
Berkeley, California

While every effort has been made to keep the content of this book accurate, the author and publisher accept no responsibility whatsoever for anyone ordering bad beer or getting messed up in any other way because of the linguistic confidence this phrase book has given them.

JMP travel guidebooks by Rick Steves

Europe 101: History and Art for the Traveler (with Gene
  Openshaw)
*Rick Steves' Mona Winks: Self-guided Tours of Europe's Top
  Museums* (with Gene Openshaw)
Rick Steves' Postcards from Europe
Rick Steves' Best of Europe
Rick Steves' Europe Through the Back Door
Rick Steves' France, Belgium & the Netherlands (with Steve
  Smith)
Rick Steves' Germany, Austria & Switzerland
Rick Steves' Great Britain & Ireland
Rick Steves' Italy
Rick Steves' Russia & the Baltics (with Ian Watson)
Rick Steves' Scandinavia
Rick Steves' Spain & Portugal
Rick Steves' London (with Gene Openshaw)
Rick Steves' Paris (with Steve Smith and Gene Openshaw)
Rick Steves' Phrase Books for: French, German, Italian,
  Spanish/Portuguese, and French/Italian/German
Asia Through the Back Door

Rick Steves' company, *Europe Through the Back Door*,
provides many services for budget travelers, including a free
quarterly newsletter/catalog, budget travel books and accessories, Eurailpasses (with free video and travel advice included),
free-spirited European tours, on-line travel tips, and a Travel
Resource Center in Edmonds, WA. For a free newsletter, call,
write, or e-mail:

Europe Through the Back Door
120 Fourth Avenue N., Box 2009
Edmonds, WA 98020 USA
Tel: 425/771-8303, Fax: 425/771-0833
Web: http://www.ricksteves.com
E-mail: rick@ricksteves.com

iv

Contents

Hi, I'm Rick Steves.

I'm the only mono-lingual speaker I know who's had the nerve to design a series of European phrase books. But that's one of the things that makes them better. You see, after 25 summers of travel through Europe, I've learned first-hand (1) what's essential for communication in another country, and (2) what's not. I've assembled the most important words and phrases in a logical, no-frills format, and I've worked with native Europeans and seasoned travelers to give you the simplest, clearest translations possible.

But this book is more than just a pocket translator. The words and phrases have been carefully selected to make you a happier, more effective budget traveler. The key to getting more out of every travel dollar is to get closer to the local people, and to rely less on entertainment, restaurants, and hotels that cater only to foreign tourists. This book will not only help you order a meal at a locals-only Parisian restaurant—it will help you talk with the family that runs the place . . . about their kids, travel dreams, politics, and favorite *fromage*. Long after your memories of *châteaux* have faded, you'll still treasure the personal encounters you had with your new French friends.

A good phrase book should help you enjoy your French experience—not just survive it—so I've added a healthy dose of humor. But please use these phrases carefully, in a self-effacing spirit. Remember that one ugly American can undo the goodwill built by dozens of culturally-sensitive ones.

To get the most out of this book, take the time to internalize and put into practice my French pronunciation tips. I've spelled out the pronunciations as if you were reading English. Don't worry too much about memorizing grammatical rules, like which gender a particular noun is—the important thing is to communicate!

You'll notice this book has a dictionary and a nifty menu decoder. You'll also find tongue twisters, gestures, international words, telephone tips, and a handy tear-out "cheat sheet." Tear it out and tuck it in your beret, so you can easily use it to memorize key phrases during otherwise idle moments. As you prepare for your trip to France, you may want to have a look at my annually-updated *Rick Steves' France* guidebook.

Your French experience will be enriched by a basic understanding of French etiquette. This causes lots of needless frustration among Americans. Here's the situation in a nutshell. Americans feel that informality is friendly, and formality is cold. The French feel that informality is rude, and formality is polite. So ironically, as the Americans and French are both doing their best to be nice, they accidentally offend one another. Remember, you're the outsider, so watch the locals and try to incorporate some French-style politeness into your routine. Walk into any shop in France and you will hear a cheery *"Bonjour, Monsieur / Madame."* As you leave, you'll hear a lilting *"Au revoir, Monsieur / Madame."* Always address a man as *Monsieur*, a woman as *Madame*, and an unmarried young woman or a girl as *Mademoiselle* (leaving this out is like addressing a French person as "Hey, you!"). For good measure, toss in *s'il vous plaît* (please) whenever you can.

So adjust those cultural blinders. If you come to France expecting rudeness, you are sure to find it. If you respect the fine points of French culture and make an attempt to speak their language, you'll find the French as warm and friendly as anyone in Europe.

My goal is to help you become a more confident, extroverted traveler. If this phrase book helps make that happen, or if you have suggestions for making it better, I'd love to hear from you. I personally read and value all feedback. My address is Europe Through the Back Door, P.O. Box 2009, Edmonds, WA 98020, tel. 425/771-8303, fax 425/771-0833, e-mail: rick@ricksteves.com.

Happy travels, and *bonne chance* (good luck) as you hurdle the language barrier!

Rick Steves

Getting Started

Challenging, romantic French

...is spoken throughout Europe and thought to be one of the most beautiful languages in the world. Half of Belgium speaks French, and French rivals English as the handiest second language in Spain, Portugal, and Italy. Even your U.S. passport is translated into French. You're probably already familiar with this poetic language. Consider: *bonjour, c'est la vie, bon appétit, merci, au revoir, bon voyage!*

As with any language, the key to communicating is to go for it with a mixture of bravado and humility. Try to sound like Maurice Chevalier or Inspector Clouseau.

French has some unusual twists to its pronunciation:

Ç sounds like S in sun.
CH sounds like SH in shine.
G usually sounds like G in get.
    But *G* followed by *E* or *I* sounds like S in treasure.
GN sounds like NI in onion.
H is always silent.
J sounds like S in treasure.
R sounds like an R being swallowed.
I sounds like EE in seed.
È and *Ê* sound like E in let.
É and *EZ* sound like AY in play.
ER, at the end of a word, sounds like AY in play.
Ô sounds like O in note.

In a Romance language, sex is unavoidable. A man is *content* (happy), a woman is *contente*. In this book, when you see a pair of words like *"content / contente,"* use the second word when talking about a woman.

French has strange-looking accents. The cedilla makes Ç sound like "s" (*façade*). The circumflex makes Ê sound like "eh" (*crêpe*), but has no effect on Â, Î, Ô, or Û. The grave accent stifles È into "eh" (*crème*), but doesn't change the stubborn À. The acute accent opens É into "ay" (*café*).

French is tricky because the spelling and pronunciation seem to have little to do with each other. *Qu'est-ce que c'est?* (What is that?) is pronounced: kehs kuh say.

The final letters of many French words are silent, so *Paris* sounds like pah-ree. The French tend to stress every syllable evenly: pah-ree. In contrast, Americans say **Par**-is, emphasizing the first syllable.

In French, if a word that ends in a consonant is followed by a word that starts with a vowel, the consonant is frequently linked with the vowel. *Mes amis* (my friends) is pronounced: may-zah-mee. Some words are linked with an apostrophe. *Ce est* (It is) becomes *C'est*, as in *C'est la vie* (That's life). *Le* and *la* (the masculine and feminine "the") are intimately connected to words starting with a vowel. *La orange* becomes *l'orange*.

French has a few sounds that are unusual in English: the French *u* and the nasal vowels. To say the French *u*, round your lips to say "oh," but say "ee." Vowels combined with either *n* or *m* are often nasal vowels. As you nasalize a vowel, let the sound come through your nose as well as your mouth. The vowel is the important thing. The *n* or *m*, represented in this book by <u>n</u> for nasal, is not pronounced.

There are a total of four nasal sounds, all contained in the phrase *un bon vin blanc* (a good white wine).

Nasal vowels:	Phonetics:	To make the sound:
un	uh<u>n</u>	nasalize the U in lung.
bon	oh<u>n</u>	nasalize the O in bone.
vin	a<u>n</u>	nasalize the A in sack.
blanc	ah<u>n</u>	nasalize the A in want.

In phonetics, *un bon vin blanc* would look like this: uh<u>n</u> boh<u>n</u> va<u>n</u> blah<u>n</u>. If you practice it, you'll learn how to say the nasal vowels . . . and order a fine wine.

Here's a guide to the rest of the phonetics in this book:

ah	like A in father.
ay	like AY in play.
eh	like E in let.
ee	like EE in seed.
ehr	sounds like "air."
ew	pucker your lips and say "ee."
g	like G in go.
or	like OR in core.
oh	like O in note.
oo	like OO in too.
s	like S in sun.
uh	like U in but.
ur	like UR in purr.
zh	like S in treasure.

French Basics

Greeting and meeting the French:

Good day.	**Bonjour.**	bohn-zhoor
Good morning.	**Bonjour.**	bohn-zhoor
Good evening.	**Bonsoir.**	bohn-swahr
Good night.	**Bonne nuit.**	buhn nwee
Hi. (informal)	**Salut.**	sah-lew
Welcome!	**Bienvenue!**	bee-an-vuh-new
Mr.	**Monsieur**	muhs-yur
Mrs.	**Madame**	mah-dahm
Miss	**Mademoiselle**	mahd-mwah-zehl
How are you?	**Comment allez-vous?**	koh-mahnt ah-lay-voo
Very well, thank you.	**Très bien, merci.**	treh bee-an mehr-see
And you?	**Et vous?**	ay voo
My name is...	**Je m'appelle...**	zhuh mah-pehl
What's your name?	**Quel est votre nom?**	kehl ay voh-truh nohn
Pleased to meet you.	**Enchanté.**	ahn-shahn-tay
Where are you from?	**D'où êtes-vous?**	doo eht voo
I am / Are you...?	**Je suis / Êtes-vous...?**	zhuh sweez / eht-vooz
...on vacation	**...en vacances**	ahn vah-kahns
...on business	**...en voyage d'affaires**	ahn voy-yahzh dah-fair
See you later.	**À bientôt.**	ah bee-an-toh
Goodbye.	**Au revoir.**	oh vwahr
Good luck!	**Bonne chance!**	buhn shahns
Have a good trip!	**Bon voyage!**	bohn voy-yahzh

Survival phrases

In 1945, American G.I.s helped liberate Paris using only these phrases. They're repeated on your tear-out cheat sheet near the end of this book.

The essentials:

Good day.	**Bonjour.**	bohn-zhoor
Do you speak English?	**Parlez-vous anglais?**	par-lay-voo ahn-glay
Yes. / No.	**Oui. / Non.**	wee / nohn
I don't speak French.	**Je ne parle pas français.**	zhuh nuh parl pah frahn-say
I'm sorry.	**Désolé.**	day-zoh-lay
Please.	**S'il vous plaît.**	see voo play
Thank you.	**Merci.**	mehr-see
No problem.	**Pas de problème.**	pah duh proh-blehm
It's good.	**C'est bon.**	say bohn
You are very kind.	**Vous êtes très gentil.**	vooz eht treh zhahn-tee
Goodbye.	**Au revoir.**	oh vwahr

Where?

Where is...?	**Où est...?**	oo ay
...a hotel	**...un hôtel**	uhn oh-tehl
...a youth hostel	**...une auberge de jeunesse**	ewn oh-behrzh duh zhuh-nehs
...a restaurant	**...un restaurant**	uhn rehs-toh-rahn
...a grocery store	**...une épicerie**	ewn ay-pee-suh-ree
...a pharmacy	**...une pharmacie**	ewn far-mah-see

6 French Basics

...a bank	...une banque	ewn bahnk
...the train station	...la gare	lah gar
...the tourist information office	...l'office du tourisme	loh-fees dew too-reez-muh
Where are the toilets?	Où sont les toilettes?	oo sohn lay twah-leht
men / women	hommes / dames	ohm / dahm

How much?

How much is it?	Combien?	kohn-bee-an
Write it?	Ecrivez?	ay-kree-vay
Cheap.	Bon marché.	bohn mar-shay
Cheaper.	Moins cher.	mwan shehr
Cheapest.	Le moins cher.	luh mwan shehr
Is it free?	C'est gratuit?	say grah-twee
Included?	Inclus?	an-klew
Do you have...?	Avez-vous...?	ah-vay-voo
Where can I buy...?	Où puis-je acheter...?	oo pwee-zhuh ah-shuh-tay
I would like...	Je voudrais...	zhuh voo-dray
We would like...	Nous voudrions...	noo voo-dree-ohn
...this.	...ceci.	suh-see
...just a little.	...un petit peu.	uhn puh-tee puh
...more.	...encore.	ahn-kor
...a ticket.	...un billet.	uhn bee-yay
...a room.	...une chambre.	ewn shahn-bruh
...the bill.	...l'addition.	lah-dee-see-ohn

How many?

one	**un**	uh<u>n</u>
two	**deux**	duh
three	**trois**	twah
four	**quatre**	kah-truh
five	**cinq**	sa<u>n</u>k
six	**six**	sees
seven	**sept**	seht
eight	**huit**	weet
nine	**neuf**	nuhf
ten	**dix**	dees

You'll find more to count on in the Numbers chapter.

When?

At what time?	**À quelle heure?**	ah kehl ur
Just a moment.	**Un moment.**	uh<u>n</u> moh-mah<u>n</u>
Now.	**Maintenant.**	ma<u>n</u>-tuh-nah<u>n</u>
soon / later	**bientôt / plus tard**	bee-a<u>n</u>-toh / plew tar
today / tomorrow	**aujourd'hui / demain**	oh-zhoor-dwee / duh-ma<u>n</u>

Be creative! You can combine these survival phrases to say: "Two, please," or "No, thank you," or "I'd like a cheap hotel," or "Cheaper, please?" Please is a magic word in any language. If you want something and you don't know the word for it, just point and say, *"S'il vous plaît"* (Please). If you know the word for what you want, such as the bill, simply say, *"L'addition, s'il vous plaît"* (The bill, please).

Struggling with French:

Do you speak English?	**Parlez-vous anglais?**	par-lay-voo ah<u>n</u>-glay
A teeny weeny bit?	**Un petit peu?**	uh<u>n</u> puh-tee puh
Please speak English.	**Parlez anglais, s'il vous plaît.**	par-lay ah<u>n</u>-glay see voo play
You speak English well.	**Vous parlez bien anglais.**	voo par-lay bee-a<u>n</u> ah<u>n</u>-glay
I don't speak French.	**Je ne parle pas français.**	zhuh nuh parl pah frah<u>n</u>-say
I speak a little French.	**Je parle un petit peu français.**	zhuh parl uh<u>n</u> puh-tee puh frah<u>n</u>-say
What is this in French?	**Qu'est-ce que c'est en français?**	kehs kuh say ah<u>n</u> frah<u>n</u>-say
Repeat?	**Répétez?**	ray-pay-tay
Speak slowly, please.	**Parlez lentement, s'il vous plaît.**	par-lay lah<u>n</u>-tuh-mah<u>n</u> see voo play
Slower.	**Plus lentement.**	plew lah<u>n</u>-tuh-mah<u>n</u>
I understand.	**Je comprends.**	zhuh koh<u>n</u>-prah<u>n</u>
I don't understand.	**Je ne comprends pas.**	zhuh nuh koh<u>n</u>-prah<u>n</u> pah
Do you understand?	**Comprenez-vous?**	koh<u>n</u>-pruh-nay-voo
Write it?	**Ecrivez?**	ay-kree-vay
Does someone here speak English?	**Il y a quelqu'un qui parle anglais?**	eel yah kehl-kuh<u>n</u> kee parl ah<u>n</u>-glay
Who speaks English?	**Qui parle anglais?**	kee parl ah<u>n</u>-glay

A French person who is asked, "Do you speak English?" assumes you mean, "Do you speak English *fluently*?" and will likely answer no. But if you just keep on struggling in

French, you'll bring out the English in most any French person.

Common questions:

How much?	**Combien?**	kohn-bee-an
How many?	**Combien?**	kohn-bee-an
How long...?	**Combien de temps...?**	kohn-bee-an duh tahn
...is the trip	**...dure le voyage**	dewr luh voy-yahzh
How many minutes?	**Combien de minutes?**	kohn-bee-an duh mee-newt
How many hours?	**Combien d'heures?**	kohn-bee-an dur
Is it far?	**C'est loin?**	say lwan
How?	**Comment?**	koh-mahn
Is it possible?	**C'est possible?**	say poh-see-bluh
Is it necessary?	**C'est nécessaire?**	say nay-suh-sair
Can you help me?	**Pouvez-vous m'aider?**	poo-vay-voo may-day
What? (didn't hear)	**Comment?**	koh-mahn
What is that?	**Qu'est-ce que c'est?**	kehs kuh say
What is better?	**Qu'est-ce qui vaut mieux?**	kehs kee voh mee-uh
What's going on?	**Qu'est-ce qui se passe?**	kehs kee suh pahs
When?	**Quand?**	kahn
What time is it?	**Quelle heure est-il?**	kehl ur ay-teel
At what time?	**À quelle heure?**	ah kehl ur
On time? Late?	**A l'heure? En retard?**	ah lur / ahn ruh-tar
When does this...?	**Ça... à quelle heure?**	sah... ah kehl ur
...open / close	**...ouvre / ferme**	oo-vruh / fehrm
Do you have...?	**Avez-vous...?**	ah-vay-voo

Can I...?	Puis-je...?	pwee-zhuh
Can we...?	Pouvons-nous...?	poo-vohn-noo
...have one	...avoir un	ahv-wahr uhn
...go free	...aller gratuitement	ah-lay grah-tweet-mahn
Where is...?	Où est...?	oo ay
Where are...?	Où sont...?	oo sohn
Where can I find / buy...?	Où puis-je trouver / acheter...?	oo pwee-zhuh troo-vay / ah-shuh-tay
Who?	Qui?	kee
Why?	Pourquoi?	poor-kwah
Why not?	Pourquoi pas?	poor-kwah pah
Yes or no?	Oui ou non?	wee oo nohn

To prompt a simple answer, ask, *"Oui ou non?"* (Yes or no?). To turn a word or sentence into a question, ask it in a questioning tone. *"C'est bon"* (It's good) becomes *"C'est bon?"* (Is it good?). An easy way to say, "Where is the toilet?" is to ask, *"Toilette?"*

La yin et yang:

cheap / expensive	bon marché / cher	bohn mar-shay / shehr
big / small	grand / petit	grahn / puh-tee
hot / cold	chaud / froid	shoh / frwah
open / closed	ouvert / fermé	oo-vehr / fehr-may
entrance / exit	entrée / sortie	ahn-tray / sor-tee
push / pull	pousser / tirer	poo-say / tee-ray
arrive / depart	arriver / partir	ah-ree-vay / par-teer
early / late	tôt / tard	toh / tar
soon / later	bientôt / plus tard	bee-an-toh / plew tar
fast / slow	vite / lent	veet / lahn

here / there	**ici / là-bas**	ee-see / lah-bah
near / far	**près / loin**	preh / lwan
indoors / outdoors	**l'intérieur / dehors**	lan-tay-ree-yoor / duh-or
good / bad	**bon / mauvais**	bohn / moh-vay
best / worst	**le meilleur / le pire**	luh meh-yur / luh peer
a little / lots	**un peu / beaucoup**	uhn puh / boh-koo
more / less	**plus / moins**	plew / mwan
mine / yours	**mien / votre**	mee-an / voh-truh
everybody / nobody	**tout le monde / personne**	too luh mohnd / pehr-suhn
easy / difficult	**facile / difficile**	fah-seel / dee-fee-seel
left / right	**à gauche / à droite**	ah gohsh / ah dwaht
up / down	**en haut / en bas**	ahn oh / ahn bah
above / below	**au-dessus / en-dessous**	oh-duh-sew / ahn-duh-soo
young / old	**jeune / vieux**	zhuhn / vee-uh
new / old	**neuve / vieux**	nuhv / vee-uh
heavy / light	**lourd / léger**	loor / lay-zhay
dark / light	**sombre / clair**	sohn-bruh / klair
happy (m), happy (f) / sad	**content, contente / triste**	kohn-tahn, kohn-tahnt / treest
beautiful / ugly	**belle / laid**	behl / leh
nice / mean	**gentil / méchant**	zhahn-tee / may-shahn
intelligent / stupid	**intelligent / stupide**	an-teh-lee-zhahn / stew-peed
vacant / occupied	**libre / occupé**	lee-bruh / oh-kew-pay
with / without	**avec / sans**	ah-vehk / sahn

Big little words:

I	**je**	zhuh
you (formal)	**vous**	voo
you (informal)	**tu**	tew
we	**nous**	noo
he	**il**	eel
she	**elle**	ehl
they	**ils**	eel
and	**et**	ay
at	**à**	ah
because	**parce que**	pars kuh
but	**mais**	may
by (via)	**par**	par
for	**pour**	poor
from	**de**	duh
here	**ici**	ee-see
if	**si**	see
in	**en**	ahn
not	**pas**	pah
now	**maintenant**	man-tuh-nahn
only	**seulement**	suhl-mahn
or	**ou**	oo
this / that	**ce / cette**	suh / seht
to	**à**	ah
very	**très**	treh

L'Alphabet:

In case you need to spell your name out loud or participate in a spelling bee...

a	ah	j	zhee	s	"s"
b	bay	k	kah	t	tay
c	say	l	"l"	u	ew
d	day	m	"m"	v	vay
e	uh	n	"n"	w	doo-bluh vay
f	"f"	o	"o"	x	"x"
g	zhay	p	pay	y	ee grek
h	ahsh	q	kew	z	zehd
i	ee	r	ehr		

Quintessentially French expressions:

Bon appétit!	boh<u>n</u> ah-pay-tee	Enjoy your meal!
Ça va?	sah vah	How are you? (informal)
Ça va.	sah vah	I'm fine. (response to Ça va?)
Ce n'est pas vrai!	suh nay pah vray	It's not true!
C'est comme ça.	say kohm sah	That's the way it is.
Comme ci, comme ça.	kohm see kohm sah	So so.
D'accord.	dah-kor	O.K.
Formidable!	for-mee-dah-bluh	Great!
Mon Dieu!	moh<u>n</u> dee-uh	My God!
Tout de suite.	toot sweet	Right away.
Voilà.	vwah-lah	Here it is.

Places in France:
If French clerks at train stations and conductors on trains don't understand your pronunciation of the name of a town, write the name on a piece of paper.

Arles	arl
Alsace	ahl-sahs
Amboise	ahm-bwahz
Annecy	ah<u>n</u>-see
Antibes	ah<u>n</u>-teeb
Arles	arl
Arromanches	ah-roh-mah<u>n</u>sh
Avignon	ah-veen-yohn
Bayeux	bah-yuh
Beaune	bohn
Beynac	bay-nak
Bordeaux	bor-doh
Calais	kah-lay
Carcassonne	kar-kah-suhn
Chambord	shah<u>n</u>-bor
Chamonix	shah-moh-nee
Chartres	shart
Chenonceau	shuh-noh<u>n</u>-soh
Cherbourg	shehr-boor
Chinon	shee-noh<u>n</u>
Collioure	kohl-yoor
Colmar	kohl-mar
Côte d'Azur	koht dah-zewr
Dijon	dee-zhoh<u>n</u>
Dordogne	dor-dohn-yuh
Giverny	zhee-vehr-nee
Grenoble	gruh-noh-bluh
Honfleur	oh<u>n</u>-floor
Le Havre	luh hah-vruh
Loire	lwahr

Lyon	lee-oh<u>n</u>
Marseille	mar-say
Mont Blanc	moh<u>n</u> blah<u>n</u>
Mont St. Michel	moh<u>n</u> sa<u>n</u> mee-shehl
Nantes	nah<u>nt</u>
Nice	nees
Normandy	nor-mah<u>n</u>-dee
Paris	pah-ree
Provence	proh-vah<u>n</u>s
Reims	ra<u>n</u>s (rhymes with France)
Rouen	roo-ah<u>n</u>
Roussillon	roo-see-yoh<u>n</u>
Sarlat	sahr-lah
Strasbourg	strahs-boorg
Verdun	vehr-duh<u>n</u>
Versailles	vehr-sigh
Villefranche	veel-frah<u>n</u>sh

French names for places:

France	**la France**	lah frah<u>n</u>s
English Channel	**la Manche**	lah mah<u>n</u>sh
England	**l'Angleterre**	lah<u>n</u>-gluh-tehr
Netherlands	**les Pays-Bas**	lay peh-ee-bah
Germany	**l'Allemagne**	lahl-mahn-yuh
Switzerland	**la Suisse**	lah swees
Austria	**l'Autriche**	loh-treesh
Spain	**l'Espagne**	luh-spahn-yuh
Italy	**l'Italie**	lee-tah-lee
Europe	**l'Europe**	lur-rohp
United States	**les Etats-Unis**	layz ay-tah-zew-nee
Canada	**le Canada**	luh kah-nah-dah
world	**le monde**	luh moh<u>n</u>d

Numbers

0	**zéro**	zay-roh
1	**un**	uh<u>n</u>
2	**deux**	duh
3	**trois**	twah
4	**quatre**	kah-truh
5	**cinq**	sa<u>n</u>k
6	**six**	sees
7	**sept**	seht
8	**huit**	weet
9	**neuf**	nuhf
10	**dix**	dees
11	**onze**	oh<u>n</u>z
12	**douze**	dooz
13	**treize**	trehz
14	**quatorze**	kah-torz
15	**quinze**	ka<u>n</u>z
16	**seize**	sehz
17	**dix-sept**	dee-seht
18	**dix-huit**	deez-weet
19	**dix-neuf**	deez-nuhf
20	**vingt**	va<u>n</u>
21	**vingt et un**	va<u>n</u>t ay uh<u>n</u>
22	**vingt-deux**	va<u>n</u>t-duh
23	**vingt-trois**	va<u>n</u>t-twah
30	**trente**	trah<u>n</u>t
31	**trente et un**	trah<u>n</u>t ay uh<u>n</u>
40	**quarante**	kah-rah<u>n</u>t
41	**quarante et un**	kah-rah<u>n</u>t ay uh<u>n</u>
50	**cinquante**	sa<u>n</u>-kah<u>n</u>t
60	**soixante**	swah-sah<u>n</u>t
70	**soixante-dix**	swah-sah<u>n</u>t-dees
71	**soixante et onze**	swah-sah<u>n</u>t ay oh<u>n</u>z
72	**soixante-douze**	swah-sah<u>n</u>t-dooz
73	**soixante-treize**	swah-sah<u>n</u>t-trehz

74	**soixante-quatorze**	swah-sah<u>n</u>t-kah-torz
75	**soixante-quinze**	swah-sah<u>n</u>t-ka<u>n</u>z
76	**soixante-seize**	swah-sah<u>n</u>t-sehz
77	**soixante-dix-sept**	swah-sah<u>n</u>t-dee-seht
78	**soixante-dix-huit**	swah-sah<u>n</u>t-deez-weet
79	**soixante-dix-neuf**	swah-sah<u>n</u>t-deez-nuhf
80	**quatre-vingts**	kah-truh-va<u>n</u>
81	**quatre-vingt-un**	kah-truh-va<u>n</u>-uh<u>n</u>
82	**quatre-vingt-deux**	kah-truh-va<u>n</u>-duh
83	**quatre-vingt-trois**	kah-truh-va<u>n</u>-twah
84	**quatre-vingt-quatre**	kah-truh-va<u>n</u>-kah-truh
85	**quatre-vingt-cinq**	kah-truh-va<u>n</u>-sa<u>n</u>k
86	**quatre-vingt-six**	kah-truh-va<u>n</u>-sees
87	**quatre-vingt-sept**	kah-truh-va<u>n</u>-seht
88	**quatre-vingt-huit**	kah-truh-va<u>n</u>-weet
89	**quatre-vingt-neuf**	kah-truh-va<u>n</u>-nuhf
90	**quatre-vingt-dix**	kah-truh-va<u>n</u>-dees
91	**quatre-vingt-onze**	kah-truh-va<u>n</u>-oh<u>n</u>z
92	**quatre-vingt-douze**	kah-truh-va<u>n</u>-dooz
93	**quatre-vingt-treize**	kah-truh-va<u>n</u>-trehz
94	**quatre-vingt-quatorze**	kah-truh-va<u>n</u>-kah-torz
95	**quatre-vingt-quinze**	kah-truh-va<u>n</u>-ka<u>n</u>z
96	**quatre-vingt-seize**	kah-truh-va<u>n</u>-sehz
97	**quatre-vingt-dix-sept**	kah-truh-va<u>n</u>-dee-seht
98	**quatre-vingt-dix-huit**	kah-truh-va<u>n</u>-deez-weet
99	**quatre-vingt-dix-neuf**	kah-truh-va<u>n</u>-deez-nuhf
100	**cent**	sah<u>n</u>
101	**cent un**	sah<u>n</u> uh<u>n</u>
102	**cent deux**	sah<u>n</u> duh
200	**deux cents**	duh sah<u>n</u>
1000	**mille**	meel
2000	**deux mille**	duh meel
2001	**deux mille un**	duh meel uh<u>n</u>
10,000	**dix mille**	dee meel
millon	**million**	uh<u>n</u> meel-yoh<u>n</u>
billion	**milliard**	meel-yar
first	**premier**	pruhm-yay

second	deuxième	duhz-yehm
third	troisième	twahz-yehm
half	demi	duh-mee
100%	cent pourcents	sah<u>n</u> poor-sah<u>n</u>
number one	numéro un	new-may-roh uh<u>n</u>

French numbering is a little quirky from the seventies through the nineties. Let's pretend momentarily that the French speak English. Instead of saying 70, 71, 72, up to 79, the French say "sixty ten," "sixty eleven," "sixty twelve" up to "sixty nineteen." Instead of saying 80, the French say "four twenties." The numbers 81 and 82 are literally "four twenty one" and "four twenty two." It gets stranger. The number 90 is "four twenty ten." To say 91, 92, up to 99, the French say "four twenty eleven," "four twenty twelve" on up to "four twenty nineteen." But take heart. If little French children can learn these numbers, so can you. Besides, didn't Abe Lincoln say, "Four score and seven..."

Money

Can you change dollars?	**Pouvez-vous changer les dollars?**	poo-vay-voo shahn-zhay lay doh-lar
What is your exchange rate for dollars...?	**Quel est le cours du dollar...?**	kehl ay luh koor dew doh-lar
...in traveler's checks	**...en chèques de voyage**	ahn shehk duh voy-yahzh
What is the commission?	**Quel est la commission?**	kehl ay lah koh-mee-see-ohn
Any extra fee?	**Il y a d'autre frais?**	eel yah doh-truh fray
I would like...	**Je voudrais...**	zhuh voo-dray
...small bills.	**...des petits billets.**	day puh-tee bee-yay
...large bills.	**...des gros billets.**	day groh bee-yay
...coins.	**...des pièces.**	day pee-ehs
...small change.	**...de la petite monnaie.**	duh lah puh-teet moh-nay
Is this a mistake?	**C'est une erreur?**	sayt ewn er-ror
I'm broke / poor / rich.	**Je suis fauché / pauvre / riche.**	zhuh swee foh-shay / poh-vruh / reesh
75 F	**soixante quinze francs**	swah-sahnt kanz frahn
50 c	**cinquante centimes**	san-kahnt sahn-teem
euro	**euro**	yoo-roh
Where is a cash machine?	**Où est un distributeur de billets?**	oo ay uhn dee-stree-bew-tur duh bee-yay

It's easy to travel throughout France without visiting a single bank by using an ATM or debit card at cash machines. You might see these words on a *distributeur de billets* (cash machine): *annuler* (cancel), *modifier* (change), *valider* (affirm).

Key money words:

bank	**banque**	bah<u>n</u>k
money	**argent**	ar-zhah<u>n</u>
change money	**changer de l'argent**	shah<u>n</u>-zhay duh lar-zhah<u>n</u>
exchange	**bureau de change**	bew-roh duh shah<u>n</u>zh
buy / sell	**acheter / vendre**	ah-shuh-tay / vah<u>n</u>-druh
commission	**commission**	koh-mee-see-oh<u>n</u>
traveler's check	**chèque de voyage**	shehk duh voy-yahzh
credit card	**carte de crédit**	kart duh kray-dee
cash advance	**crédit de caisse**	kray-dee duh kehs
cash machine	**distributeur de billets**	dee-stree-bew-tur duh bee-yay
cashier	**caisse**	kehs
cash	**liquide**	lee-keed
bills	**billets**	bee-yay
coins	**pièces**	pee-ehs
receipt	**reçu**	ruh-sew

At French banks, you may encounter a security door that allows one person to enter at a time. Push the *entrez* (enter) button, then *attendez* (wait), and *voilà*, the door opens.

French *francs* (F) are divided into 100 *centimes* (c). There are about 5.5 francs in a dollar, so divide prices in francs by five to get a rough estimate of the price in dollars. Forty francs = about $8 (actually $7.30). France has many different coins. The 10F and 20F coins are thick, valuable, and two-colored (gold and silver). None of this will matter after 2002

when the common currency throughout Europe's 11-country
Euroland will be the euro (€).

Time

What time is it?	Quelle heure est-il?	kehl ur ay-teel
It's...	Il est...	eel ay
...8:00.	...huit heures.	weet ur
...16:00.	...seize heures.	sehz ur
...4:00 in the afternoon.	...quatre heures de l'après-midi.	kah-truh ur duh lah-preh-mee-dee
...10:30 (in the evening).	...dix heures et demie (du soir).	deez ur ayd-mee (dew swahr)
...a quarter past nine.	...neuf heures et quart.	nuhv ur ay kar
...a quarter to eleven.	...onze heures moins le quart.	ohnz ur mwan luh kar
...noon / midnight.	...midi / minuit.	mee-dee / meen-wee
...sunrise.	...l'aube.	lohb
...sunset.	...le coucher de soleil.	luh koo-shay duh soh-lay
...early / late.	...tôt / tard.	toh / tar
...on time.	...a l'heure.	ah lur

In France, the 24-hour clock (or military time) is used by
hotels and stores, and for train, bus, and ferry schedules.
Informally, the French use the 24-hour clock and "our clock"
interchangeably—17:00 is also 5:00 *de l'après-midi* (in the
afternoon). The greeting *"Bonjour"* (Good day) turns to
"Bonsoir" (Good evening) at sundown.

Timely words:

minute	**minute**	mee-newt
hour	**heure**	ur
morning	**matin**	mah-ta<u>n</u>
afternoon	**après-midi**	ah-preh-mee-dee
evening	**soir**	swahr
night	**nuit**	nwee
day	**jour**	zhoor
today	**aujourd'hui**	oh-zhoor-dwee
yesterday	**hier**	yehr
tomorrow	**demain**	duh-ma<u>n</u>
tomorrow morning	**demain matin**	duh-ma<u>n</u> mah-ta<u>n</u>
anytime	**n'importe quand**	na<u>n</u>-port kah<u>n</u>
immediately	**immédiatement**	ee-may-dee-aht-mah<u>n</u>
in one hour	**dans une heure**	dah<u>n</u>z ewn ur
every hour	**toutes les heures**	toot layz ur
every day	**tous les jours**	too lay zhoor
last	**dernier**	dehrn-yay
this	**ce**	suh
next	**prochain**	proh-sha<u>n</u>
May 15	**le quinze mai**	luh ka<u>n</u>z may
high / low season	**haute / basse saison**	oht / bahs say-zoh<u>n</u>
in the future	**dans l'avenir**	dah<u>n</u> lah-vah<u>n</u>-eer
in the past	**dans le passé**	dah<u>n</u> luh pah-say
week	**semaine**	suh-mehn
Monday	**lundi**	luh<u>n</u>-dee
Tuesday	**mardi**	mar-dee
Wednesday	**mercredi**	mehr-kruh-dee
Thursday	**jeudi**	zhuh-dee
Friday	**vendredi**	vahn-druh-dee
Saturday	**samedi**	sahm-dee
Sunday	**dimanche**	dee-mah<u>n</u>sh

month	**mois**	mwah
January	**janvier**	zhahn-vee-yay
February	**février**	fay-vree-yay
March	**mars**	mars
April	**avril**	ahv-reel
May	**mai**	may
June	**juin**	zhwan
July	**juillet**	zhwee-yay
August	**août**	oot
September	**septembre**	sehp-tahn-bruh
October	**octobre**	ohk-toh-bruh
November	**novembre**	noh-vahn-bruh
December	**décembre**	day-sahn-bruh
year	**année**	ah-nay
spring	**printemps**	pran-tahn
summer	**été**	ay-tay
fall	**automne**	oh-tuhn
winter	**hiver**	ee-vehr

TIME

French holidays and happy days:

holiday	**jour férié**	zhoor fay-ree-ay
national holiday	**fête nationale**	feht nah-see-oh-nahl
Independence Day (July 14)	**le quatorze juillet**	luh kah-torz zhwee-yay
school holidays	**vacances scolaires**	vah-kahns skoh-lehr
religious holiday	**fête religieuse**	feht ruh-lee-zhuhz
Is it a holiday today / tomorrow?	**C'est un jour férié aujourd'hui / demain?**	say tuhn zhoor fay-ree-ay oh-zhoor-dwee / duh-man
What is the holiday?	**C'est quel jour férié?**	say kehl zhoor fay-ree-ay
Easter	**Pâques**	pahk
Merry Christmas!	**Joyeux Noël!**	zhwah-yuh noh-ehl
Happy new year!	**Bonne année!**	buhn ah-nay

| Happy wedding anniversary! | **Bon anniversaire de mariage!** | bohn ah-nee-vehr-sehr duh mah-ree-yahzh |
| Happy birthday! | **Bon anniversaire!** | bohn ah-nee-vehr-sehr |

The French sing "Happy birthday" to the same tune we do. Here are the words: *Joyeux anniversaire, joyeux anniversaire, joyeux anniversaire* (fill in name), *nos voeux les plus sincères.*

Other celebrations include May 1 (Labor Day), May 8 (Liberation Day), and August 15 (Assumption of Mary). France's biggest holiday is on July 14, Bastille Day. Festivities begin on the evening of the 13th and rage throughout the country.

If a holiday falls on a Thursday, many get Friday off as well: the Friday is called *le pont*, or the bridge, between the holiday and the weekend. On school holidays (*vacances scolaires*), families head for the beach, jamming resorts.

Transportation

TRANSPORTATION

Trains

Is this the line for...?	**C'est la file pour...?**	say lah feel poor
...tickets	**...les billets**	lay bee-yay
...reservations	**...les réservations**	lay ray-zehr-vah-see-ohn
How much is the fare to...?	**C'est combien pour allez à...?**	say kohn-bee-an poor ah-lay ah
A ticket to ___.	**Un billet pour ___.**	uhn bee-yay poor
When is the next train?	**Le prochain train part á quelle heure?**	luh proh-shan tran par ah kehl ur
I'd like to leave...	**Je voudrais partir...**	zhuh voo-dray par-teer
I'd like to arrive...	**Je voudrais arriver...**	zhuh voo-dray ah-ree-vay
...by ___.	**...à ___.**	ah
...in the morning.	**...le matin.**	luh mah-tan
...in the afternoon.	**...l'après-midi.**	lah-preh-mee-dee
...in the evening.	**...le soir.**	luh swahr
Is there a...?	**Y a-t-il un...?**	ee ah-teel uhn
...earlier train	**...train plus tôt**	tran plew toh
...later train	**...train plus tard**	tran plew tar
...overnight train	**...train de nuit**	tran duh nwee

...supplement	...supplément	sew-play-mahn
Does my railpass cover the supplement?	Le supplément est inclus dans mon railpass?	luh sew-play-mahn ay an-klew dahn mohn rayl-pahs
Is there a discount for...?	Y a-t-il une réduction pour les...?	ee ah-teel ewn ray-dewk-see-ohn poor lay
...youth	...jeunes	zhuhn
...seniors	...gens âgée	zhahn ah-zhay
Is a reservation required?	Une réservation est-elle nécessaire?	ewn ray-zehr-vah-see-ohn ay-tehl nay-suh-sair
I'd like to reserve...	Je voudrais réserver...	zhuh voo-dray ray-zehr-vay
...a seat.	...une place.	ewn plahs
...a berth.	...une couchette.	ewn koo-sheht
...a sleeper.	...un compartiment privé.	uhn kohn-par-tuh-mahn pree-vay
Where does (the train) leave from?	Il part d'où?	eel par doo
What track?	Quelle voie?	kehl vwah
On time? Late?	A l'heure? En retard?	ah lur / ahn ruh-tar
When will it arrive?	Il va arriver à quelle heure?	eel vah ah-ree-vay ah kehl ur
Is it direct?	C'est direct?	say dee-rehkt
Must I transfer?	Faut-il prendre une correspondance?	foh-teel prahn-druh ewn kor-rehs-pohn-dahns
When? / Where?	À quelle heure? / Où?	ah kehl ur / oo
Which train to...?	Quel train pour...?	kehl tran poor
Which train car to...?	Quelle voiture pour...?	kehl vwah-tewr poor
Where is first class?	Où se trouve la première classe?	oo suh troov lah pruhm-yehr klahs
...front	...à l'avant	ah lah-vahn

...middle	...au milieu	oh meel-yuh
...back	...au fond	oh foh<u>n</u>
Is (the seat) free?	C'est libre?	say lee-bruh
That's my seat.	C'est ma place.	say mah plahs
Save my place?	Gardez ma place?	gar-day mah plahs
Where are you going?	Où allez-vous?	oo ah-lay-voo
I'm going to...	Je vais à...	zhuh vay ah
Tell me when to get off?	Dites-moi quand je descends?	deet-mwah kah<u>n</u> zhuh day-sah<u>n</u>
Is there a train to / from the airport?	Est-ce qu'il y a un train à / de l'aéroport?	ehs keel yah uhn tra<u>n</u> ah / duh lah-ay-roh-por

TRANSPORTATION

Ticket talk:

ticket window	guichet	gee-shay
reservations window	comptoir des réservations	koh<u>n</u>-twahr day ray-zehr-vah-see-oh<u>n</u>
national / international	en France / internationaux	ah<u>n</u> frah<u>n</u>s / een-tehr-nah-see-oh<u>n</u>-oh
ticket	billet	bee-yay
one way	aller simple	ah-lay sa<u>n</u>-pluh
roundtrip	aller-retour	ah-lay-ruh-toor
first class	première classe	pruhm-yehr klahs
second class	deuxième classe	duhz-yehm klahs
non-smoking	non fumeur	noh<u>n</u> few-mur
reduced fare	tarif réduit	tah-reef ray-dwee
validate	composter	koh<u>n</u>-poh-stay
schedule	horaire	oh-rair
departure	départ	day-par

direct	**direct**	dee-rehkt
transfer	**correspondance**	kor-rehs-poh<u>n</u>-dah<u>ns</u>
with supplement	**avec supplément**	ah-vehk sew-play-mah<u>n</u>
reservation	**réservation**	ray-zehr-vah-see-oh<u>n</u>
seat...	**place...**	plahs
...by the window	**...à la fenêtre**	ah lah fuh-neh-truh
...on the aisle	**...au couloir**	oh kool-wahr
berth...	**couchette...**	koo-sheht
...upper	**...supérieure**	sew-pay-ree-ur
...middle	**...milieu**	meel-yuh
...lower	**...inférieure**	a<u>n</u>-fay-ree-ur
refund	**remboursement**	rah<u>n</u>-boor-suh-mah<u>n</u>

You must *composter* (validate) your train ticket (and any reservation) prior to boarding the train. Look for the waist-high orange machines on the platform and insert your ticket and reservation separately—watch others and imitate.

At the train station:

French State Railways	**SNCF**	S N say F
train station	**gare**	gar
train information	**renseignements**	rah<u>n</u>-sehn-yuh-mah<u>n</u>
	SCNF	S N say F
train	**train**	tra<u>n</u>
high-speed train	**TGV**	tay zhay vay
arrival	**arrivée**	ah-ree-vay
departure	**départ**	day-par
delay	**retard**	ruh-tar
toilet	**toilette**	twah-leht
waiting room	**salle d'attente**	sahl dah-tah<u>n</u>t

lockers	**consigne automatique**	kohn-seen-yuh oh-toh-mah-teek
baggage check room	**consigne de bagages**	kohn-seen-yuh duh bah-gahzh
lost and found office	**bureau des objets trouvés**	bew-roh dayz ohb-zhay troo-vay
tourist information	**office du tourisme**	oh-fees dew too-reez-muh
to the platforms	**accès aux quais**	ahk-seh oh kay
platform	**quai**	kay
track	**voie**	vwah
train car	**voiture**	vwah-tewr
dining car	**voiture restaurant**	vwah-tewr rehs-toh-rahn
sleeper car	**wagon-lit**	vah-gohn-lee
conductor	**conducteur**	kohn-dewk-tur

Major rail lines in France

French schedules use the 24-hour clock. It's like American time until noon. After that, subtract twelve and add p.m. So 13:00 is 1 p.m., 20:00 is 8 p.m., and 24:00 is midnight. If your train is scheduled to depart at 00:01, it'll leave one minute after midnight.

Train schedules show blue (quiet), white (normal), and red (peak and holiday) times. You can save money if you get the blues (travel during off-peak hours).

Reading train and bus schedules:

à, pour	to
arrivée	arrival
de	from
départ	departure
dimanche	Sunday
en retard	late
en semaine	workdays (Monday-Saturday)
et	and
heure	hour
horaire	timetable
jour férié	holiday
jours	days
jusqu'à	until
la semaine	weekdays
par	via
pas	not
samedi	Saturday
sauf	except
seulement	only
tous	every
tous les jours	daily
vacances	holidays
voie	track
1-5	Monday-Friday
6, 7	Saturday, Sunday

TRANSPORTATION

Buses and subways:

How do I get to...?	**Comment aller à...?**	koh-mahn tah-lay ah
Which bus to...?	**Quel bus pour...?**	kehl bews poor
Does it stop at...?	**Est-ce qu'il s'arrête à...?**	ehs keel sah-reht ah
Which stop for...?	**Quel arrêt pour...?**	kehl ah-reh poor

Which direction for...?	**Quelle direction pour...?**	kehl dee-rehk-see-ohn poor
Must I transfer?	**Faut-il prendre une correspondance?**	foh-teel prahn-druh ewn kor-rehs-pohn-dahns
How much is a ticket?	**Combien le ticket?**	kohn-bee-an luh tee-kay
Where can I buy a ticket?	**Où puis-je acheter un ticket?**	oo pwee-zhuh ah-shuh-tay uhn tee-kay
When does the... leave?	**Quand est-ce que le... part?**	kahn ehs kuh luh... par
...first / next / last	**...premier / prochain / dernier**	pruhm-yay / proh-shan / dehrn-yay
...bus / subway	**...bus / métro**	bews / may-troh
What's the frequency per hour / day?	**Combien de fois par heure / jour?**	kohn-bee-an duh fwah par ur / zhoor
I'm going to...	**Je vais à...**	zhuh vay ah
Tell me when to get off?	**Dites-moi quand je descends?**	deet-mwah kahn zhuh day-sahn
Is there a bus to / from the airport?	**Est-ce qu'il y a un bus à / de l'aéroport?**	ehs keel yah uhn bews ah / duh lah-ay-roh-por

Key bus and subway words:

ticket	**ticket**	tee-kay
city bus	**bus**	bews
long-distance bus	**car**	kar
bus stop	**arrêt de bus**	ah-reh duh bews
bus station	**gare routière**	gar root-yehr
subway	**métro**	may-troh
subway map	**plan du métro**	plahn dew may-troh
subway entrance	**l'entrée du métro**	lahn-tray dew may-troh
subway stop	**station de métro**	stah-see-ohn duh may-troh
subway exit	**sortie**	sor-tee

direct	**direct**	dee-rehkt
connection	**correspondance**	kor-rehs-pohn-dahns
pick-pocket	**voleur**	voh-loor
10 tickets	**carnet**	kar-nay

In Paris, you'll save money by buying a *carnet* (batch of ten tickets) at virtually any *métro* station. The tickets, which are sharable, are valid on the buses, métro, and R.E.R. (underground rail lines) within the city limits.

Taxis:

Taxi!	**Taxi!**	tahk-see
Can you call a taxi?	**Pouvez-vous appeler un taxi?**	poo-vay-vooz ah-puh-lay uhn tahk-see
Where is a taxi stand?	**Où est une station de taxi?**	oo ay ewn stah-see-ohn duh tahk-see
Are you free?	**Libre?**	lee-bruh
Occupied.	**Occupé.**	oh-kew-pay
How much will it cost to go to...?	**C'est combien pour aller à...?**	say kohn-bee-an poor ah-lay ah
...the airport	**...l'aéroport**	lah-ay-roh-por
...the train station	**...la gare**	lah gar
...this address	**...cette adresse**	seht ah-drehs
It's too much.	**C'est trop.**	say troh
This is all I have.	**C'est tout ce que j'ai.**	say too suh kuh zhay
Can you take ___ people?	**Pouvez-vous prendre ___ passagers?**	poo-vay-voo prahn-druh ___ pah-sah-zhay
Any extra fee?	**Il y a d'autre frais?**	eel yah doh-truh fray
The meter, please.	**Le compteur, s'il vous plaît.**	luh kohn-tur see voo play
Where is the meter?	**Où est le compteur?**	oo ay luh kohn-tur

I'm in a hurry.	**Je suis pressé.**	zhuh swee preh-say
The most direct route.	**La route la plus directe.**	lah root lah plew dee-rehkt
Slow down.	**Ralentissez.**	rah-lahn-tee-say
If you don't slow down, I'll throw up.	**Si vous ne ralentissez pas, je vais vomir.**	see voo nuh rah-lahn-tee-say pah, zhuh vay voh-meer
Stop here.	**Arrêtez-vous ici.**	ah-reh-tay-voo ee-see
Can you wait?	**Pouvez-vous attendre?**	poo-vay-vooz ah-tahn-druh
I'll never forget this ride.	**Je ne vais jamais oublier cette promenade.**	zhuh nuh vay zhah-may oo-blee-yay seht prohm-nahd
Where did you learn to drive?	**Où avez-vous appris à conduire?**	oo ah-vay-voo ah-preez ah kohn-dweer
I'll only pay what's on the meter.	**Je paie seulement ce qui est indiqué.**	zhuh pay suhl-mahn suh kee ayt an-dee-kay
My change, please.	**La monnaie, s'il vous plaît.**	lah moh-nay see voo play
Keep the change.	**Gardez la monnaie.**	gar-day lah moh-nay

So you'll know what to expect, ask about typical taxi fares at your hotel. Fares go up at night and on Sundays, and drivers always charge for loading baggage in the trunk. Your fare can nearly double if you're taking a short trip with lots of bags. Tipping (about 5%) is optional.

Rental wheels:

I'd like to rent...	**Je voudrais louer...**	zhuh voo-dray loo-ay
...a car.	**...une voiture.**	ewn vwah-tewr
...a station wagon.	**...un break.**	uhn brayk

...a van.	...un van.	uhn vahn
...a motorcycle.	...une motocyclette.	ewn moh-toh-see-kleht
...a motor scooter.	...un vélomoteur.	uhn vay-loh-moh-tur
...a bicycle.	...un vélo.	uhn vay-loh
...a mountain bike.	...un VTT.	uhn vay-tay-tay
...the Concorde.	...le Concorde.	luh kohn-kord
How much per...?	Combien par...?	kohn-bee-an par
...hour	...heure	ur
...day	...jour	zhoor
...week	...semaine	suh-mehn
Unlimited mileage?	Kilométrage illimité?	kee-loh-may-trazh eel-lee-mee-tay
I brake for bakeries.	Je m'arrête à chaque boulangerie.	zhuh mah-reht ah shahk boo-lahn-zhuh-ree
Is there...?	Est-ce qu'il ya...?	ehs keel yah
...a helmet	...un casque	uhn kahsk
...a discount	...une réduction	ewn ray-dewk-see-ohn
...a deposit	...une caution	ewn koh-see-ohn
...insurance	...une assurance	ewn ah-sewr-rahns
When do I bring it back?	A quelle heure faut-il le ramener?	ah kehl ur foh-teel luh rah-muh-nay

Driving:

gas station	station service	stah-see-ohn sehr-vees
The nearest gas station?	La plus proche station service?	lah plew prohsh stah-see-ohn sehr-vees
Is it self-service?	C'est libre service?	say lee-bruh sehr-vees
Fill the tank.	Faites le plein.	feht luh plan

I need...	Il me faut...	eel muh foh
...gas.	...de l'essence.	duh leh-sah<u>ns</u>
...unleaded.	...sans plomb.	sah<u>n</u> ploh<u>n</u>
...regular.	...normale.	nor-mahl
...super.	...du super.	dew sew-pehr
...diesel.	...gazoil.	gah-zoyl
Check...	Vérifiez...	vay-ree-fee-ay
...the oil.	...l'huile.	lweel
...the air in the tires.	...la pression dans les pneus.	lah pruh-see-oh<u>n</u> dah<u>n</u> lay puh-nuh
...the radiator.	...le radiateur.	lah rahd-yah-tur
...the battery.	...la batterie.	lah bah-tuh-ree
...the fuses.	...les fusibles.	lay few-zee-bluh
...the sparkplugs.	...les bougies.	lay boo-zhee
...headlights.	...les phares.	lay fahr
...tail lights.	...les feux arrières.	lay fuh ah-ree-ehr
...directional signal.	...le clignotant.	luh klee-noh-tah<u>n</u>
...car mirror.	...la rétroviseur.	lah ray-troh-vee-zur
...the fanbelt.	...la courroie du ventilateur.	lah koor-wah dew vah<u>n</u>-tee-lah-tur
...the brakes.	...les freins.	lay fra<u>n</u>
...my pulse.	...mon poul.	moh<u>n</u> pool

The cheapest gas in France is sold in *hypermarché* (supermarket) parking lots. Rather than dollars and gallons, pumps will read francs and liters (basically 5.5 francs in a dollar, and 4 liters in a gallon).

Car trouble:

accident	**accident**	ahk-see-dah<u>n</u>
breakdown	**en panne**	ah<u>n</u> pahn
funny noise	**bruit curieux**	brwee kew-ree-uh
electrical problem	**problème d'électricité**	proh-blehm day-lehk-tree-see-tay
flat tire	**pneu crevé**	puh-nuh kruh-vay
The battery is dead.	**La batterie est foutu.**	lah bah-tuh-ree ay foo-tew
It won't start.	**Elle ne démarre pas.**	ehl nuh day-mar pah
This doesn't work.	**Ça ne marche pas.**	sah nuh marsh pah
It's overheating.	**Le moteur surchauffe.**	luh moh-tur sewr-shohf
I need a...	**Il me faut un...**	eel muh foh uh<u>n</u>
...tow truck.	**...dépanneur.**	day-pah-nur
...mechanic.	**...mécanicien.**	may-kah-nee-see-a<u>n</u>
...stiff drink.	**...bon coup.**	boh<u>n</u> koo

For help with repair, look up "Repair" under Shopping.

Parking:

parking garage	**garage de stationment**	gah-rahzh duh stah-see-ohn-mah<u>n</u>
parking meter	**horodateur**	oh-roh-dah-tur
Where can I park?	**Où puis-je me garer?**	oo pwee-zhuh muh gah-ray
Is parking nearby?	**Y a-t-il un parking près d'ici?**	ee ah-teel uh<u>n</u> par-keeng preh dee-see

TRANSPORTATION

Can I park here?	**Puis-je me garer ici?**	pwee-zhuh muh gah-ray ee-see
How long can I park here?	**Je peux me garer ici pour combien de temps?**	zhuh puh muh gah-ray ee-see poor koh<u>n</u>-bee-a<u>n</u> duh tah<u>n</u>
Must I pay to park here?	**Dois-je payer pour me garer ici?**	dwah-zhuh pay-yay poor muh gah-ray ee-see
Is this a safe place to park?	**C'est prudent de se garer ici?**	say prew-dah<u>n</u> duh suh gah-ray ee-see

Many French cities use remote meters for curb-side parking. After you park, look for a meter at the street corner and buy a ticket to place on the dash. If you're not certain you need a ticket, look at the dashboards of cars parked nearby. If they have tickets, you'll need one, too. Ask a local for help finding the *horodateur* (parking meter).

Finding your way:

I am going to...	**Je vais à...**	zhuh vay ah
How do I get to...?	**Comment aller à...?**	koh-mah<u>n</u> tah-lay ah
Do you have...?	**Avez-vous...?**	ah-vay-voo
...a city map	**...un plan de la ville**	uh<u>n</u> plah<u>n</u> duh lah veel
...a road map	**...une carte routière**	ewn kart root-yehr
How many minutes...?	**Combien de minutes...?**	koh<u>n</u>-bee-a<u>n</u> duh mee-newt
How many hours...?	**Combien d'heures...?**	koh<u>n</u>-bee-a<u>n</u> dur
...on foot	**...à pied**	ah pee-yay
...by bicycle	**...à bicyclette**	ah bee-see-kleht
...by car	**...en voiture**	ah<u>n</u> vwah-tewr
How many kilometers to...?	**Combien de kilomètres à...?**	koh<u>n</u>-bee-a<u>n</u> duh kee-loh-meh-truh ah

What's the...	**Quelle est la...**	kehl eh lah...
route to Paris?	**route pour Paris?**	root poor pah-ree
...best	**...meilleure**	meh-yur
...fastest	**...plus directe**	plew dee-rehkt
...most interesting	**...plus intéressante**	plewz an-tay-reh-sahnt
Point it out?	**Montrez-moi?**	mohn-tray mwah
I'm lost.	**Je suis perdu.**	zhuh swee pehr-dew
Where am I?	**Où suis-je?**	oo swee-zhuh
Who am I?	**Qui suis-je?**	kee swee-zhuh
Where is...?	**Où est...?**	oo ay
The nearest...?	**Le plus proche...?**	luh plew prohsh
Where is this address?	**Où se trouve cette adresse?**	oo suh troov seht ah-drehs

TRANSPORTATION

Key route-finding words:

city map	**plan de la ville**	plahn duh lah veel
road map	**carte routière**	kart root-yehr
downtown	**centre-ville**	sahn-truh-veel
straight ahead	**tout droit**	too dwah
left / right	**à gauche / à droite**	ah gohsh / ah dwaht
first / next	**premier / prochain**	pruhm-yay / proh-shan
intersection	**carrefour**	kar-foor
roundabout	**rondpoint**	rohn-pwan
ring road	**rocade**	roh-kahd
stoplight	**feu**	fuh
square	**place**	plahs
street	**rue**	rew
bridge	**pont**	pohn
tunnel	**tunnel**	tew-nehl
highway	**grande route**	grahnd root
national highway	**route nationale**	root nah-see-oh-nahl

freeway	**autoroute**	oh-toh-root
north / south	**nord / sud**	nor / sewd
east / west	**est / ouest**	ehs / wehs

Along the *autoroute*, electronic signs flash messages to let you know what's ahead: *bouchon* (traffic jam), *circulation* (traffic), and *fluide* (no traffic). The shortest distance between any two points is the *autoroute*, but the tolls add up. You'll travel cheaper, but slower, on a *route nationale*.

If you see the flashing lights of a patrol car, try this handy phrase: *"Pardon, je suis touriste."* (Sorry, I'm a tourist.) Or, for the adventurous: *"Si vous n'aimez pas ma conduite, vous n'avez qu'à descendre du trottoir."* (If you don't like how I drive, get off the sidewalk.)

Reading road signs:

attention travaux	workers ahead
autres directions	other directions (follow when leaving a town)
céder le passage	yield
centre ville	to the center of town
déviation	detour
entrée	entrance
péage	toll
prochaine sortie	next exit
ralentir	slow down
réservé aux piétons	pedestrians only
sans issue	dead end
sauf riverains	local access only
sens unique	one-way street
sortie	exit

stationnement interdit	no parking
stop	stop
toutes directions	all directions (follow when leaving a town)
travaux	construction
virages	curves

Here are the standard symbols you'll see:

STOP	No Entry For Cars	All Vehicles Prohibited	No Entry	Speed Limit (in km)	Yield	No Passing	Danger	Parking

Other signs you may bump into:

à louer	for rent or for hire
à vendre	for sale
chambre libre	vacancy
chien méchant	mean dog
complet	no vacancy
dames	women
danger	danger
défence de fumer	no smoking
défense de toucher	do not touch
défense d'entrer	keep out
eau non potable	undrinkable water
entrée libre	free admission
entrée interdite	no entry
en panne	out of service
fermé	closed
fermé pour restauration	closed for restoration

fermeture annuelle	closed for vacation
guichet	ticket window
hommes	men
hors service	out of service
interdit	forbidden
occupé	occupied
ouvert	open
ouvert de... à...	open from... to...
poussez / tirez	push / pull
prudence	caution
solde	sale
sortie de secours	emergency exit
tirez / poussez	pull / push
toilettes	toilets
WC	toilet

Sleeping

Places to stay:

hotel	**hôtel**	oh-tehl
small hotel	**pension**	pah<u>n</u>-see-oh<u>n</u>
room in private home	**chambre d'hôte**	shah<u>n</u>-bruh doht
youth hostel	**auberge de jeunesse**	oh-behrzh duh zhuh-nehs
country home rental	**gîte**	zheet
vacancy	**chambre libre**	shah<u>n</u>-bruh lee-bruh
no vacancy	**complet**	koh<u>n</u>-play

Reserving a room:

If you reserve your room by phone, a good time to call is the morning of the day you plan to arrive. To reserve by fax, use the nifty form in the appendix.

Hello.	**Bonjour.**	boh<u>n</u>-zhoor
Do you speak English?	**Parlez-vous anglais?**	par-lay-voo ah<u>n</u>-glay
Do you have a room...?	**Avez-vous une chambre...?**	ah-vay-voo ewn shah<u>n</u>-bruh
...for one person	**...pour une personne**	poor ewn pehr-suhn
...for two people	**...pour deux personnes**	poor duh pehr-suhn
...for tonight	**...pour ce soir**	poor suh swahr
...for two nights	**...pour deux nuits**	poor duh nwee
...for this Friday	**...pour ce vendredi**	poor suh vah<u>n</u>-druh-dee
...for June 21	**...pour le vingt et un juin**	poor luh va<u>n</u>t ay uh<u>n</u> zhwa<u>n</u>
Yes or no?	**Oui ou non?**	wee oo noh<u>n</u>

I'd like...	**Je voudrais...**	zhuh voo-dray
...a private bathroom.	**...une salle de bains.**	ewn sahl duh ban
...your cheapest room.	**...la chambre la moins chère.**	lah shahn-bruh lah mwan shehr
...___ beds for ___ people in ___ rooms.	**...___ lits par ___ personnes dans ___ chambres.**	___ lee par ___ pehr-suhn dahn ___ shahn-bruh
How much is it?	**Combien?**	kohn-bee-an
Anything cheaper?	**Rien de moins cher?**	ree-an duh mwan shehr
I'll take it.	**Je la prends.**	zhuh lah prahn
My name is...	**Je m'appelle...**	zhuh mah-pehl
I'll stay...	**Je reste...**	zhuh rehst
We'll stay...	**Nous restons...**	noo rehs-tohn
...___ nights.	**...___ nuits.**	___ nwee
I'll come...	**J'arrive...**	zhah-reev
We'll come...	**Nous arrivons...**	nooz ah-ree-vohn
...in one hour.	**...dans une heure.**	dahnz ewn ur
...before 16:00.	**...avant seize heures.**	ah-vahn sehz ur
...Friday before 6 p.m.	**...vendredi avant six heures du soir.**	vahn-druh-dee ah-vahn seez ur dew swahr
Thank you.	**Merci.**	mehr-see

Getting specific:

I'd like a room...	**Je voudrais une chambre...**	zhuh voo-dray ewn shahn-bruh
...with / without / and	**...avec / sans / et**	ah-vehk / sahn / ay
...toilet	**...WC**	vay say
...sink and toilet	**...cabinet de toilette**	kah-bee-nay duh twah-leht
...shower	**...douche**	doosh

...shower and toilet	...salle d'eau	sahl doh
...shower down the hall	...douche sur le palier	doosh sewr luh pahl-yay
...bathtub and toilet	...salle de bain	sahl duh ban
...double bed	...grand lit	grahn lee
...twin beds	...deux petits lits, lits jumeaux	duh puh-tee lee, lee zhew-moh
...balcony	...balcon	bahl-kohn
...view	...vue	vew
...only a sink	...lavabo seulement	lah-vah-boh suhl-mahn
...on the ground floor	...au rez-de-chaussée	oh ray-duh-shoh-say
...television	...télévision	tay-lay-vee-zee-ohn
...telephone	...téléphone	tay-lay-fohn
Is there an elevator?	Y a-til un ascenseur?	ee ah-teel uhn ah-sahn-sur
We arrive Monday, depart Wednesday.	Nous arrivons lundi, nous partons mercredi.	nooz ah-ree-vohn luhn-dee, noo par-tohn mehr-kruh-dee
I'll sleep anywhere. I'm desperate.	Je vais dormir n'importe où. Je suis désespéré.	zhuh vay dor-meer nan-port oo. zhuh swee day-zuh-spay-ray
I have a sleeping bag.	J'ai un sac de couchage.	zhay uhn sahk duh koo-shahzh
Will you call another hotel?	Pouvez-vous contacter un autre hôtel?	poo-vay-voo kohn-tahk-tay uhn oh-truh oh-tehl

SLEEPING

Offering some of the best budget beds in Europe, French hotels are rated from one to four stars (check the blue & white plaque by the front door). For budget travelers, one or two stars is the best value. Prices vary widely under one roof. A room with a double bed (*grand lit*) is cheaper than a room with twin beds (*deux petits lits*), and a bathroom with a shower (*salle d'eau*) is cheaper than a bathroom with a bathtub (*salle de bain*). Rooms with just a toilet and sink (*cabinet de toilette*, abbreviated *C. de T*) are even cheaper, and a room with only a sink (*lavabo seulement*) is the cheapest.

Confirming, changing, and canceling reservations:
You can use this template for your telephone call.

I have a reservation.	**J'ai une réservation.**	zhay ewn ray-zehr-vah-see-oh<u>n</u>
My name is...	**Je m'appelle...**	zhuh mah-pehl
I'd like to... my reservation.	**Je voudrais... ma réservation.**	zhuh voo-dray... mah ray-zehr-vah-see-oh<u>n</u>
...confirm	**...confirmer**	koh<u>n</u>-feer-may
...reconfirm	**...réconfirmer**	ray-koh<u>n</u>-feer-may
...cancel	**...annuler**	ah-noo-lay
...change	**...modifier**	moh-dee-fee-ay
The reservation is / was for...	**La réservation est / était pour...**	lah ray-zehr-vah-see-oh<u>n</u> ay / ay-tay poor
...one person / two persons	**...une personne / deux personnes**	ewn pehr-suhn / duh pehr-suhn
...today / tomorrow	**...aujourd'hui / demain**	oh-zhoor-dwee / duh-ma<u>n</u>
...August 13	**...le treize août**	luh trehz oot
...one night / two nights	**...une nuit / deux nuits**	ewn nwee / duh nwee
Did you find my reservation?	**Avez-vous trouvé ma réservation?**	ah-vay-voo troo-vay mah ray-zehr-vah-see-oh<u>n</u>

I'd like to arrive instead on...	Je préfère arriver le...	zhuh pray-fehr ah-ree-vay luh
Is everything O.K.?	Ça va marcher?	sah vah mar-shay
Thank you. I'll see you then.	Merci. À bientôt.	mehr-see ah bee-an-toh
I'm sorry I need to cancel.	Je suis désolé, car il faut que j'annule.	zhuh swee day-zoh-lay kar eel foh kuh zhah-nool

Nailing down the price:

How much is...?	Combien...?	kohn-bee-an
...a room for ___ people	...une chambre pour ___ personnes	ewn shahn-bruh poor ___ pehr-suhn
...your cheapest room	...la chambre la moins chère	lah shahn-bruh lah mwan shehr
Is breakfast included?	Petit déjeuner compris?	puh-tee day-zhuh-nay kohn-pree
Is breakfast required?	Le petit déjeuner est obligatoire?	luh puh-tee day-shuh-nay ayt oh-blee-gah-twahr
How much without breakfast?	Combien sans le petit déjeuner?	kohn-bee-an sahn luh puh-tee day-zhuh-nay
Complete price?	Tout compris?	too kohn-pree
Is it cheaper if I stay ___ nights?	C'est moins cher si je reste ___ nuits?	say mwan shehr see zhuh rehst ___ nwee
I'll stay ___ nights.	Je vais rester ___ nuits.	zhuh vay rehs-tay ___ nwee

Choosing a room:

| Can I see the room? | Puis-je voir la chambre? | pwee-zhuh vwahr lah shahn-bruh |

Show me another room?	**Montrez-moi une autre chambre?**	mohn-tray-mwah ewn oh-truh shahn-bruh
Do you have something...?	**Avez-vous quelque chose de...?**	ah-vay-voo kehl-kuh shohz duh
...larger / smaller	**...plus grand / moins grand**	plew grahn / mwan grahn
...better / cheaper	**...meilleur / moins cher**	meh-yur / mwan shehr
...brighter	**...plus clair**	ploo klair
...in the back	**...derrière**	dehr-yehr
...quieter	**...plus tranquille**	plew trahn-keel
I'll take it.	**Je la prends.**	zhuh lah prahn
My key, please.	**La clé, s'il vous plaît.**	lah klay see voo play
Sleep well.	**Dormez bien.**	dor-may bee-an
Good night.	**Bonne nuit.**	buhn nwee

Hotel help:

I'd like...	**Je voudrais...**	zhuh voo-dray
...a / another	**...un / un autre**	uhn / uhn oh-truh
...towel.	**...serviette de bain.**	sehrv-yeht duh ban
...pillow.	**...oreiller.**	oh-reh-yay
...fluffy pilllow.	**...coussin.**	koo-san
...clean sheets.	**...draps propres.**	drah proh-pruh
...blanket.	**...couverture.**	koo-vehr-tewr
...glass.	**...verre.**	vehr
...sink stopper.	**...bouchon pour le lavabo.**	boo-shohn poor luh lah-vah-boh
...soap.	**...savon.**	sah-vohn
...toilet paper.	**...papier hygiénique.**	pahp-yay ee-zhay-neek

...crib.	...berceau.	behr-soh
...cot.	...lit de camp.	lee duh kahn
...roll-away bed.	...lit pliant.	lee plee-ahn
...different room.	...autre chambre.	oh-truh shahn-bruh
...silence.	...silence.	see-lahns
Where can I wash / hang my laundry?	Où puis-je faire / étendre ma lessive?	oo pwee-zhuh fair / ay-tahn-druh mah luh-seev
I'd like to stay another night.	Je voudrais rester encore une nuit.	zhuh voo-dray rehs-tay ahn-kor ewn nwee
Where can I park?	Je me gare où?	zhuh muh gar oo
What time do you lock up?	Vous fermez à quelle heure?	voo fehr-may ah kehl ur
What time is breakfast?	Le petit déjeuner est servi à quelle heure?	luh puh-tee day-zhuh-nay ay sehr-vee ah kehl ur
Please wake me at 7:00.	Réveillez-moi à sept heures, si'l vous plaît.	ray-veh-yay-mwah ah seht ur see voo play

If you'd rather not struggle all night with a log-style French pillow, check in the closet to see if there's a fluffier American-style pillow, or ask for a *"coussin"* (koo-san).

Hotel hassles:

Come with me.	Venez avec moi.	vuh-nay ah-vehk mwah
I have a problem in my room.	J'ai un problème dans ma chambre.	zhay uhn proh-blehm dahn mah shahn-bruh
bad odor	mauvaise odeur	moh-vehz oh-dur
bugs	insectes	an-sehkt
mice	souris	soo-ree
prostitutes	prostituées	proh-stee-tew-ay

50 Sleeping

The bed is too soft / hard.	Le lit est trop mou / dur.	luh lee eh troh moo / dewr
I'm covered with bug bites.	Je suis couvert de piqures d'insectes.	zhuh swee koo-vehr duh pee-kewr dan-sehkt
Lamp...	Lampe...	lahmp
Lightbulb...	Ampoule...	ahn-pool
Electrical outlet...	Prise...	preez
Key...	Clé...	klay
Lock...	Serrure...	suh-roor
Window...	Fenêtre...	fuh-neh-truh
Faucet...	Robinet...	roh-bee-nay
Sink...	Lavabo...	lah-vah-boh
Toilet...	Toilette...	twah-leht
Shower...	Douche...	doosh
...doesn't work.	...ne marche pas.	nuh marsh pah
There is no hot water.	Il n'y a plus d'eau chaude.	eel nee yah plew doh shohd
When is the water hot?	L'eau sera chaude à quelle heure?	loh suh-rah shohd ah kehl ur

Checking out:

I leave...	Je pars...	zhuh par
We leave...	Nous partons...	noo par-tohn
...today / tomorrow.	...aujourd'hui / demain.	oh-zhoor-dwee / duh-man
...very early.	...très tôt.	treh toh
When is check-out time?	Quelle est l'heure limite d'occupation?	kehl ay lur lee-meet doh-kew-pah-see-ohn
Can I pay now?	Puis-je régler la note?	pwee-zhuh ray-glay lah noht

The bill, please.	**La note, s'il vous plaît.**	lah noht see voo play
Credit card O.K.?	**Carte de crédit O.K.?**	kart duh kray-dee "O.K."
I slept like a baby.	**J'ai dormi comme un enfant.**	zhay dor-mee kohm uhn ahn-fahn
Everything was great.	**C'était super.**	say-tay sew-pehr
Will you call my next hotel for me?	**Pouvez-vous contacter mon prochain hôtel pour moi?**	poo-vay-voo kohn-tahk-tay mohn proh-shan oh-tehl poor mwah
Can I...?	**Puis-je...?**	pwee-zhuh
Can we...?	**Pouvons-nous...?**	poo-vohn-noo
...leave baggage here until ___	**...laisser les baggages ici jusqu'à ___**	lay-say lay bah-gahzh ee-see zhews-kah

SLEEPING

Camping:

campsite	**emplacement**	ahn-plahs-mahn
tent	**tente**	tahnt
camping	**camping**	kahn-peeng
The nearest campground?	**Le plus proche camping?**	luh plew prohsh kahn-peeng
Can I...?	**Puis-je...?**	pwee-zhuh
Can we...?	**Pouvons-nous...?**	poo-vohn-noo
...camp here for one night	**...camper ici pour une nuit**	kahn-pay ee-see poor ewn nwee
Are showers included?	**Les douches sont comprises?**	lay doosh sohn kohn-preez
shower token	**jeton**	zhuh-tohn

In some French campgrounds and hostels, you need to buy a *jeton* (token) to activate a hot shower. To avoid a sudden cold rinse, buy two *jetons* before getting undressed.

Laundry:

self-service laundry	**lavarie automatique**	lah-vah-ree oh-toh-mah-teek
wash / dry	**laver / sécher**	lah-vay / say-shay
washer / dryer	**machine à laver / machine à sécher**	mah-sheen ah lah-vay / mah-sheen ah say-shay
detergent	**détergent**	day-tehr-zhan
token	**jeton**	zhuh-tohn
whites / colors	**blancs / coleurs**	blahn / koh-lur
delicates	**délicats**	day-lee-kah
handwash	**laver à la main**	lah-vay a lah man
How does this work?	**Ça march comment?**	sah marsh koh-mahn
Where is the soap?	**Où se trouve la lessive?**	oo suh troov lah luh-seev
I need change.	**Il me faut de la monnaie.**	eel muh foh duh lah moh-nay
full-service laundry	**blanchisserie**	blahn-shee-suh-ree
Same-day service?	**Service la même jour?**	sehr-vees lah mehm zhoor
By when do I need to drop off my clothes?	**Quand est-ce que je dois déposer mon linge?**	kahn ehs kuh zhuh dwah day-poh-zay mohn lanzh
When will my clothes be ready?	**Quand est-ce que mon linge sera prêt?**	kahn ehs kuh mohn lanzh suh-rah preh
Dried?	**Séché?**	say-shay
Folded?	**Plie?**	plee-ay

Eating

EATING

Finding a restaurant:

Where's a good... restaurant?	**Où se trouve un bon restaurant...?**	oo suh troov uhn bohn rehs-toh-rahn
...cheap	**...bon marché**	bohn mar-shay
...local-style	**...cuisine régionale**	kwee-zeen ray-zhee-oh-nahl
...untouristy	**...pas touristique**	pah too-ree-steek
...Chinese	**...chinois**	sheen-wah
...fast food	**...fast food**	fahst food
...self-service	**...libre service**	lee-bruh sehr-vees
with terrace	**avec terrace**	ah-vehk tehr-rahs
with candles	**avec bougies**	ah-vehk boo-zhee
romantic	**romantique**	roh-mahn-teek
moderately-priced	**prix modéré**	pree moh-day-ray
to splurge	**faire une folie**	fehr ewn foh-lee

Getting a table and menu:

Waiter.	**Monsieur.**	muhs-yur
Waitress.	**Mademoiselle, Madame.**	mahd-mwah-zehl, mah-dahm
I'd like...	**Je voudrais...**	zhuh voo-dray
...a table for one / two.	**...une table pour un / deux.**	ewn tah-bluh poor uhn / duh
...non-smoking.	**...non fumeur.**	nohn few-mur
...just a drink.	**...une consommation seulement.**	ewn kohn-soh-mah-see-ohn suhl-mahn
...a snack.	**...un snack.**	uhn snahk
...just a salad.	**...qu'une salade.**	kewn sah-lahd
...to see the menu.	**...voir la carte.**	vwahr lah kart

...to order.	...commander.	koh-mahn-day
...to eat.	...manger.	mahn-zhay
...to pay.	...payer.	pay-yay
...to throw up.	...vomir.	voh-meer
What do you recommend?	Qu'est-ce que vous recommandez?	kehs kuh voo ruh-koh-mahn-day
What's your favorite?	Quel est votre plat favori?	kehl eh voh-truh plah fah-voh-ree
Is it...?	C'est...?	say
...good	...bon	bohn
...expensive	...cher	shehr
...light	...léger	lay-zhay
...filling	...copieux	kohp-yuh
What's cheap and filling?	Qu'est-ce qu'il y a de bon marché et de copieux?	kehs keel yah duh bohn mar-shay ay duh kohp-yuh
What is fast?	Qu'est-ce qui est déjà préparé?	kehs kee ay day-zhah pray-pah-ray
What is local?	Qu'est-ce que vous avez de la région?	kehs kuh vooz ah-vay duh lah ray-zhee-ohn
What is that?	Qu'est-ce que c'est?	kehs kuh say
Do you have...?	Avez-vous...?	ah-vay-vooz
...an English menu	...une carte en anglais	ewn kart ahn ahn-glay
...a children's portion	...une assiette d'enfant	ewn ahs-yeht dahn-fahn

While the slick self-service restaurants are easy to use, you'll often eat better for the same money in a good little family bistro.

The menu:

menu	**carte**	kart
special of the day	**plat du jour**	plah dew zhoor
fast service special	**formule rapide**	for-mewl rah-peed
fixed-price meal	**menu, prix fixe**	muh-new, pree feeks
breakfast	**petit déjeuner**	puh-tee day-zhuh-nay
lunch	**déjeuner**	day-zhuh-nay
dinner	**dîner**	dee-nay
specialty of the house	**spécialité de la maison**	spay-see-ah-lee-tay duh lah may-zohn
appetizers	**hors-d'oeuvre**	or-duh-vruh
bread	**pain**	pan
salad	**salade**	sah-lahd
soup	**soupe**	soop
first course	**entrée**	ahn-tray
main course	**plat principal**	plah pran-see-pahl
meat	**viande**	vee-ahnd
poultry	**volaille**	voh-ligh
seafood	**fruits de mer**	frwee duh mehr
vegetables	**légumes**	lay-gewm
cheese	**fromage**	froh-mahzh
dessert	**dessert**	duh-sehr
beverages	**boissons**	bwah-sohn
beer	**bière**	bee-ehr
wine	**vin**	van
service included	**service compris**	sehr-vees kohn-pree
service not included	**service non compris**	sehr-vees nohn kohn-pree
with / and / or / without	**avec / et / ou / sans**	ah-vehk / ay / oo / sahn

French cuisine is sightseeing for your tastebuds. Restaurants normally serve from 12:00 to 14:00, and from 19:00 until about 22:00. The menu is posted right on the front door or window, and "window shopping" for your meal is a fun, important part of the experience. In France, a menu is a *carte*, and a fixed-price meal is a *menu*. Many cafés offer fixed-price meals such as a *plat du jour* or *menu touristique*—you'll get your choice of an appetizer, entrée, and dessert at a set price. *Service compris (s.c.)* means the tip is included. For a complete culinary language guide, travel with the excellent Marling French Menu Master.

Dietary restrictions:

I'm allergic to...	**Je suis allergique à...**	zhuh sweez ah-lehr-zheek ah
I cannot eat...	**Je ne mange pas de...**	zhuh nuh mah<u>n</u>zh pah duh
...dairy products.	**...produits laitiers.**	proh-dwee lay-tee-yay
...meat / pork.	**...viande / porc.**	vee-ah<u>n</u>d / por
...salt / sugar.	**...sel / sucre.**	sehl / sew-kruh
I'm a diabetic.	**Je suis diabétique.**	zhuh swee dee-ah-bay-teek
No fat.	**Sans matières grasses.**	sah<u>n</u> maht-yehr grahs
Low-fat meal.	**La cuisine minceur.**	lah kwee-zeen ma<u>n</u>-sur
Low cholesterol?	**Maigre? Light?**	may-gruh / "light"
No caffeine.	**Décaféiné.**	day-kah-fay-nay
No alcohol.	**Sans alcool.**	sah<u>n</u>z ahl-kohl
I'm a...	**Je suis...**	zhuh swee
...male vegetarian.	**...végétarien.**	vay-zhay-tah-ree-a<u>n</u>
...female vegetarian.	**...végétarienne.**	vay-zhay-tah-ree-ehn

EATING

...strict vegetarian.	...végétarien rigoureux.	vay-zhay-tah-ree-an ree-goo-ruh
...carnivore.	...carnivore.	kar-nee-vor
...big eater.	...gourmand.	goor-mahn

Tableware and condiments:

plate	assiette	ahs-yeht
extra plate	une assiette de plus	ewn ahs-yeht duh plew
napkin	serviette	sehrv-yeht
silverware	couverts	koo-vehr
knife	couteau	koo-toh
fork	fourchette	foor-sheht
spoon	cuillère	kwee-yehr
cup	tasse	tahs
glass	verre	vehr
carafe	carafe	kah-rahf
water	l'eau	loh
bread	pain	pan
butter	beurre	bur
margarine	margarine	mar-gah-reen
salt / pepper	sel / poivre	sehl / pwah-vruh
sugar	sucre	sew-kruh
artificial sweetener	édulcorant	ay-dewl-koh-rahn
honey	miel	mee-ehl
mustard	moutarde	moo-tard
mayonnaise	mayonnaise	mah-yuh-nehz
ketchup	ketchup	"ketchup"

Restaurant requests and regrets:

A little.	Un peu.	uhn puh
More.	Encore.	ahn-kor
Another.	Un autre.	uhn oh-truh
The same.	La même chose.	lah mehm shohz

I did not order this.	Ce n'est pas ce que j'ai commandé.	suh nay pah suh kuh zhay koh-mahn-day
Is it included with the meal?	C'est inclus avec le repas?	say an-kloo ah-vehk luh ruh-pah
I'm in a hurry.	Je suis pressé.	zhuh swee preh-say
I must leave at...	Je dois partir a...	zhuh dwah par-teer ah
Will the food be ready soon?	Ce sera prêt bientôt?	suh suh-rah preh bee-an-toh
I've changed my mind.	J'ai changé d'avis.	zhay shahn-zhay dah-vee
Can I get it "to go?"	Pour emporter?	poor ahn-por-tay
This is...	C'est...	say
...dirty.	...sale.	sahl
...greasy.	...graisseux.	gray-suh
...too salty.	...trop salé.	troh sah-lay
...undercooked.	...pas assez cuit.	pah ah-say kwee
...overcooked.	...trop cuit.	troh kwee
...inedible.	...immangeable.	an-mahn-zhah-bluh
...cold.	...froid.	frwah
Heat this up?	Le chauffage marche?	luh shoh-fahzh marsh
Enjoy your meal!	Bon appétit!	bohn ah-pay-tee
Enough.	Assez.	ah-say
Finished.	Terminé.	tehr-mee-nay
Do any of your customers return?	Avez-vous des clients qui reviennent?	ah-vay-voo day klee-ahn kee ruh-vee-an
Yuck!	Pouah!	pwah
Delicious!	Délicieux!	day-lee-see-uh
Magnificent!	Magnifique!	mahn-yee-feek

EATING

60 Eating

| My compliments to the chef! | **Mes compliments au chef!** | may kohn-plee-mahn oh shehf |

Paying for your meal:

The bill, please.	**L'addition, s'il vous plaît.**	lah-dee-see-ohn see voo play
Together.	**Ensemble.**	ahn-sahn-bluh
Separate checks.	**Notes séparées.**	noht say-pah-ray
Credit card O.K.?	**Carte de crédit O.K.?**	kart duh kray-dee "O.K."
Is service included?	**Le service est compris?**	luh sehr-vees ay kohn-pree
This is not correct.	**Ce n'est pas exact.**	suh nay pah ehg-zahkt
Explain this?	**Expliquez ça?**	ehk-splee-kay sah
What if I wash the dishes?	**Si je lave la vaiselle moi-même?**	see zhuh lahv lah vay-sehl mwah-mehm
Keep the change.	**Gardez la monnaie.**	gar-day lah moh-nay
This is for you.	**C'est pour vous.**	say poor voo

In France, slow service is good service. Out of courtesy, your waiter will not bring your bill until you ask for it. It's polite to summon your waiter by saying, *"S'il vous plaît"* (please). While a service charge is included in the bill, it's polite to round up (to a maximum of 5%) if the service was good, helpful, and friendly.

What's for breakfast?:

breakfast	**petit déjeuner**	puh-tee day-zhuh-nay
bread	**pain**	pan
roll	**petit pain**	puh-tee pan
little loaf of bread	**baguette**	bah-geht

toast	**toast**	tohst
butter	**beurre**	bur
jelly	**confiture**	koh<u>n</u>-fee-tewr
pastry	**pâtisserie**	pah-tee-suh-ree
croissant	**croissant**	kwah-sah<u>n</u>
cheese	**fromage**	froh-mahzh
yogurt	**yaourt**	yah-oort
cereal	**céréale**	say-ray-ahl
milk	**lait**	lay
hot cocoa	**chocolat chaud**	shoh-koh-lah shoh
fruit juice	**jus de fruit**	zhew duh frwee
orange juice (fresh)	**jus d'orange (frais)**	zhew doh-rah<u>n</u>zh (fray)
coffee / tea (see Drinking)	**café / thé**	kah-fay / tay
Is breakfast included in the room cost?	**Est-ce que le petit déjeuner est compris?**	ehs kuh luh puh-tee day-zhuh-nay ay koh<u>n</u>-pree

What's not for breakfast:

omelet	**omelette**	oh-muh-leht
eggs	**des oeufs**	dayz uh
fried eggs	**oeufs au plat**	uh oh plah
scrambled eggs	**oeufs brouillés**	uh broo-yay
boiled egg...	**oeuf à la coque...**	uhf ah lah kohk
...soft / hard	**...mollet / dur**	moh-lay / dewr
ham	**jambon**	zhah<u>n</u>-boh<u>n</u>

French hotel breakfasts are small, expensive, and often
optional. They normally include coffee and a fresh *croissant*

or a chunk of *baguette* with butter and jelly. Being a juice and cheese man, I keep a liter box of O.J. in my room for a morning eye-opener and a wedge of "Laughing Cow" cheese in my bag for a moo-vable feast. You can also save money by breakfasting at a *bar* or *café*, where it's acceptable to bring in a croissant from the neighboring *boulangerie* (bakery).

Snacks and quick lunches:

crepe	**crêpe**	krehp
buckwheat crepe	**galette**	gah-leht
omelet	**omelette**	oh-muh-leht
quiche...	**quiche...**	keesh
...with cheese	**...au fromage**	oh froh-mahzh
...with ham	**...au jambon**	oh zhah<u>n</u>-boh<u>n</u>
...with mushrooms	**...aux champignons**	oh shah<u>n</u>-peen-yoh<u>n</u>
...with bacon, cheese and onions	**...lorraine**	lor-rehn
paté	**pâté**	pah-tay
onion tart	**tarte à l'oignon**	tart ah loh-yoh<u>n</u>
cheese tart	**tarte au fromage**	tart oh froh-mahzh

Light meals are quick and easy at *cafés* and *bars* throughout France. A *salade, crêpe, quiche,* or *omelette* is a fairly cheap way to fill up, even in Paris. Each can be made with various extras like ham, cheese, mushrooms, and so on. *Crêpes* come in dinner or dessert varieties.

Sandwiches:

I'd like a sandwich.	**Je voudrais un sandwich.**	zhuh voo-dray uh<u>n</u> sah<u>n</u>d-weech
toasted ham and cheese sandwich	**croque monsieur**	krohk muhs-yur
toasted ham, cheese & fried egg sandwich	**croque madame**	krohk mah-dahm
cheese	**fromage**	froh-mahzh
tuna	**thon**	toh<u>n</u>
chicken	**poulet**	poo-lay
turkey	**dinde, dindon**	dan<u>d</u>, da<u>n</u>-doh<u>n</u>
ham	**jambon**	zhah<u>n</u>-boh<u>n</u>
salami	**salami**	sah-lah-mee
boiled egg	**oeuf à la coque**	uhf ah lah kohk
garnished with veggies	**crudités**	krew-dee-tay
lettuce	**laitue**	lay-too
tomato	**tomates**	toh-maht
onions	**oignons**	oh-yoh<u>n</u>
mustard	**moutarde**	moo-tard
mayonnaise	**mayonnaise**	mah-yuh-nehz

Sandwiches, as well as small quiches, often come ready-made at *boulangeries* (bakeries).

Soups and salads:

soup (of the day)	**soupe (du jour)**	soop (dew zhoor)
broth	**bouillon...**	boo-yoh<u>n</u>
...chicken	**...de poulet**	duh poo-lay
...beef	**...de boeuf**	duh buhf
...with noodles	**...aux nouilles**	oh noo-ee

...with rice	...au riz	oh ree
thick vegetable soup	potage de légumes	poh-tahzh duh lay-gewm
onion soup	soupe à l'oignon	soop ah lohn-yohn
shellfish chowder	bisque	beesk
seafood stew	bouillabaisse	boo-yah-behs
salad...	salade...	sah-lahd
...green / mixed	...verte / mixte	vehrt / meekst
...of goat cheese	...au chevre chaud	oh sheh-vruh shoh
...chef's	...composée	kohn-poh-zay
...seafood	...oceane	oh-shee-ahn
...veggie	...crudités	krew-dee-tay
...with ham / cheese / egg	...avec jambon / fromage / oeuf	ah-vehk zhahn-bohn / froh-mahzh / uh
lettuce	laitue	lay-too
tomatoes	tomates	toh-maht
cucumber	concombre	kohn-kohn-bruh
oil / vinegar	huile / vinaigre	weel / vee-nay-gruh
dressing on the side	la sauce à part	lah sohs ah par
What is in this salad?	Qu'est-ce qu'il y a dans cette salade?	kehs keel yah dahn seht sah-lahd

Salads are usually served with a *vinaigrette* dressing.

Seafood:

seafood	fruits de mer	frwee duh mehr
assorted sea-food	assiette de fruits de mer	ahs-yeht duh frwee duh mehr
fish	poisson	pwah-sohn
cod	cabillaud	kah-bee-yoh

salty cod	**morue**	moh-rew
salmon	**saumon**	soh-moh<u>n</u>
trout	**truite**	trweet
tuna	**thon**	toh<u>n</u>
herring	**hareng**	ah-rah<u>n</u>
sardines	**sardines**	sar-deen
anchovies	**anchois**	ah<u>n</u>-shwah
clams	**palourdes**	pah-loord
mussels	**moules**	mool
oysters	**huîtres**	wee-truh
scallops	**coquilles**	koh-keel
shrimp	**crevettes**	kruh-veht
prawns	**scampi**	skah<u>n</u>-pee
crab	**crabe**	krahb
lobster	**homard**	oh-mar
squid	**calmar**	kahl-mar
Where did this live?	**D'où est-ce que ça vient?**	doo ehs kuh sah vee-a<u>n</u>
Just the head, please.	**Seulement la tête, s'il vous plaît.**	suhl-mah<u>n</u> lah teht see voo play

Poultry and meat:

poultry	**volaille**	voh-ligh
chicken	**poulet**	poo-lay
turkey	**dinde, dindon**	da<u>nd</u>, da<u>n</u>-doh<u>n</u>
duck	**canard**	kah-nar
meat	**viande**	vee-ah<u>n</u>d
beef	**boeuf**	buhf
roast beef	**rosbif**	rohs-beef
beef steak	**bifteck**	beef-tehk
flank steak	**faux-filet**	foh-fee-lay
ribsteak	**entrecôte**	ah<u>n</u>-truh-koht
mixed grill	**grillades**	gree-yahd

EATING

meat stew	ragoût	rah-goo
veal	veau	voh
cutlet	côtelette	koh-tuh-leht
pork	porc	por
ham	jambon	zhahn-bohn
sausage	saucisse	soh-sees
lamb	agneau	ahn-yoh
bunny	lapin	lah-pan
snails	escargots	ehs-kar-goh
frog legs	cuisses de grenouilles	kwees duh greh-noo-ee
How long has this been dead?	Il est mort depuis longtemps?	eel ay mor duh-pwee lohn-tahn

Worth avoiding:

These are the cheapest items on a menu—for good reason.

brains	cervelle	sehr-vehl
calf pancreas	ris de veau	ree duh voh
horse meat	viande de cheval	vee-ahnd duh shuh-vahl
intestines	andouillette	ahn-doo-yeht
liver	foie	fwah
tongue	langue	lahng
tripe	tripes	treep

How food is prepared:

hot / cold	chaud / froid	shoh / frwah
raw / cooked	cru / cuit	krew / kwee
assorted	assiette, variés	ahs-yeht, vah-ree-ay
baked	cuit au four	kweet oh foor
boiled	bouilli	boo-yee
fillet	filet	fee-lay
fresh	frais	fray
fried	frit	free
grilled	grillé	gree-yay

homemade	fait à la maison	fay ah lah may-zohn
microwave	four à micro-ondes	foor ah mee-kroh-ohnd
mild	doux	doo
mixed	mixte	meekst
poached	poché	poh-shay
roasted	rôti	roh-tee
sautéed	sauté	soh-tay
smoked	fumé	few-may
spicy hot	piquant	pee-kahn
steamed	à la vapeur	ah lah vah-pur
stuffed	farci	far-see
sweet	doux	doo
topped with cheese	gratinée	grah-tee-nay

Avoiding mis-steaks:

raw	cru	krew
very rare	bleu	bluh
rare	saignant	sayn-yahn
medium	à point	ah pwan
well-done	bien cuit	bee-an kwee
very well-done	très bien cuit	treh bee-an kwee

By American standards, the French undercook meats. In France, rare (*saignant*) is nearly raw, medium (*à point*) is rare, and well-done (*bien cuit*) is medium.

French specialties by region
Each region is followed by the name of a local city (in parentheses) and the region's specialities.

Alps (Chamonix): Try *raclette* (melted cheese over potatoes and meats) and *fondue Savoyarde* (cheese fondue).

Alsace (Colmar): Flavored by German heritage, Alsace is

known for *choucroute* (sauerkraut and sausage), *tarte à l'oignon* (onion tart), *tarte flambée* (thin quiche) and *baeckeanoffe* (stew of onions, meat, and potatoes).

Burgundy (Beaune): This wine region excels in *coq au vin* (chicken with wine sauce), *boeuf bourgignon* (beef stew cooked with wine, bacon, onions and mushrooms), *oeufs en meurette* (eggs poached in red wine), *escargots* (snails), and *jambon persillé* (ham with garlic and parsley).

Languedoc (Carcassonne): Try the hearty *cassoulet* (white bean, duck, and sausage stew), *canard* (duck), and *cargolade* (snail, lamb, and sausage stew).

Loire Valley (Amboise): Savor the fresh *truite* (trout), *veau* (veal), *rillettes* (cold minced pork paté), *fromage du chèvre* (goat cheese), *aspèrges* (asparagus), and *champignons* (mushrooms).

Normandy (Bayeux): Munch some *moules* (mussels) and *escalope Normande* (veal in cream sauce). Swallow some *cidre* (apple cider) or *calvados* (apple brandy).

Périgord (Sarlat): The food is ducky. Try the *carnard* (duck), *pâté de foie gras* (goose liver paté), *pommes sarladaise* (potatoes fried in duck fat), *truffes* (truffles, earthy mushrooms), and anything with *noix* (walnuts).

Provence (Avignon): Sample the *soupe au pistou* (vegetable soup with garlic, cheese, and basil), *ratatouille* (casserole of eggplant, zucchini, tomatoes, onions and green peppers), *brandade* (salted cod in garlic cream), and *tapenade* (a spread of pureed olives, garlic, and anchovies).

Riviera (Nice): Dive into *bouillabaisse* (seafood stew), *bourride* (creamy fish soup), *salade niçoise* (salad with potatoes, tomatoes, olives, tuna, and anchovies), and *pan bagna* (a salade niçoise on a bun).

French cooking styles and sauces:

aïoli	garlic mayonnaise
Anglaise	boiled
Béarnaise	sauce of egg yolks, butter, tarragon, white wine, and shallots
beurre blanc	sauce of butter, white wine, and shallots
Bourguignon	cooked in red wine
forestière	with mushrooms
gratinée	topped with cheese, then broiled
Hollandaise	sauce of butter and egg yolks
jardinière	with vegetables
meunière	coated with flour and fried in butter
Normande	cream sauce
Provençale	with tomatoes, garlic, olive oil, and herbs
nouvelle cuisine	a blend of fresh ingredients: appealing, low in fat, and very expensive

Veggies, beans, rice, and pasta:

vegetables	**légumes**	lay-gewm
mixed vegetables	**légumes variés**	lay-gewm vah-ree-ay
with vegetables	**garni**	gar-nee
raw veggie salad	**crudités**	krew-dee-tay
artichoke	**artichaut**	ar-tee-shoh
asparagus	**aspèrges**	ah-spehrzh
beans	**haricots**	ah-ree-koh

beets	betterave	beh-teh-rahv
broccoli	brocoli	broh-koh-lee
cabbage	chou	shoo
carrots	carottes	kah-roht
cauliflower	chou-fleur	shoo-flur
corn	maïs	mah-ees
cucumber	concombre	kohn-kohn-bruh
eggplant	aubergine	oh-behr-zheen
French fries	pommes frites	pohm freet
garlic	ail	ah-ee
green beans	haricots verts	ah-ree-koh vehr
leeks	poireaux	pwah-roh
lentils	lentilles	lahn-teel
mushrooms	champignons	shahn-peen-yohn
olives	olives	oh-leev
onions	oignons	ohn-yohn
pasta	pâtes	paht
peas	pois	pwah
pepper...	poivron...	pwah-vrohn
...green / red / hot	...vert / rouge / épicé	vehr / roozh / ay-pee-say
pickles	cornichons	kor-nee-shohn
potato	pomme de terre	pohm duh tehr
rice	riz	ree
spaghetti	spaghetti	spah-geh-tee
spinach	épinards	ay-pee-nar
tomatoes	tomates	toh-maht
zucchini	courgette	koor-zheht

Say cheese:

cheese...	fromage...	froh-mahzh
...mild	...doux	doo
...sharp	...fort	for
...goat	...chèvre	sheh-vruh
...bleu	...bleu	bluh
...herbs	...aux herbes	oh ehrb
...cream	...à la crème	ah lah krehm
...of the region	...de la région	duh lah ray-zhee-oh<u>n</u>
Swiss cheese	gruyère, emmenthal	grew-yehr, eh-mehn-tahl
Laughing Cow	La vache qui rit	lah vahsh kee ree
cheese platter	le plâteau de fromages	luh plah-toh duh froh-mahzh
May I taste a little?	Je peux goûter un peu?	zhuh puh goo-tay uh<u>n</u> puh

In France, the cheese course is served just before (or instead of) dessert. It not only helps with digestion, it gives you a great opportunity to sample the tasty regional cheeses. You've heard of *camembert* and *brie*. *Port Salut* comes in a sweet, soft wedge and *roquefort* is strong and blue-veined. *Fromage aux cindres* (cheese with cinders) is ash-ually better than it sounds. Visit a *fromagerie* (cheese shop) and experiment. Ask for a *fromage de la région* (of the region), and specify mild, sharp, goat, or bleu (see list above).

Fruits and nuts:

almond	**amande**	ah-mah<u>n</u>d
apple	**pomme**	pohm
apricot	**abricot**	ah-bree-koh
banana	**banane**	bah-nahn
berries	**baies**	bay
melon	**melon**	muh-loh<u>n</u>
cherry	**cerise**	suh-reez
chestnut	**marron, chataîgne**	mah-roh<u>n</u>, shah-tayn
coconut	**noix de coco**	nwah duh koh-koh
date	**datte**	daht
fig	**figue**	feeg
fruit	**fruit**	frwee
grapefruit	**pamplemousse**	pah<u>n</u>-pluh-moos
grapes	**raisins**	ray-za<u>n</u>
hazelnut	**noisette**	nwah-zeht
lemon	**citron**	see-troh<u>n</u>
orange	**orange**	oh-rah<u>n</u>zh
peach	**pêche**	pehsh
peanut	**cacahuete**	kah-kah-weet
pear	**poire**	pwahr
pineapple	**ananas**	ah-nah-nah
pistachio	**pistache**	pee-stahsh
plum	**prune**	prewn
prune	**pruneau**	prew-noh
raspberry	**framboise**	frah<u>n</u>-bwahz
strawberry	**fraise**	frehz
tangerine	**mandarine**	mah<u>n</u>-dah-reen
walnut	**noix**	nwah
watermelon	**pastèque**	pah-stehk

Just desserts:

dessert	**dessert**	duh-sehr
cake	**gâteau**	gah-toh
ice cream	**glace**	glahs
scoop of ice cream	**coupe de glace**	koop du glahs
sherbet	**sorbet**	sor-bay
fruit cup	**salade de fruits**	sah-lahd duh frwee
tart	**tartelette**	tar-tuh-leht
pie	**tarte**	tart
whipped cream	**crème chantilly**	krehm shahn-tee-yee
pastry	**pâtisserie**	pah-tee-suh-ree
fruit pastry	**chausson**	shoh-sohn
chocolate-filled pastry	**pain au chocolat**	pan oh shoh-koh-lah
buttery cake	**madeleine**	mah-duh-lehn
crepes	**crèpes**	krehp
sweet crepes	**crèpes sucres**	krehp sew-kruh
cookies	**petits gâteaux**	puh-tee gah-toh
candy	**bonbons**	bohn-bohn
low calorie	**bas en calories**	bah ahn kah-loh-ree
homemade	**fait à la maison**	fay ah lah may-zohn
Exquisite!	**Exquis!**	ehk-skee

Crème de la crème:

crème brulée	rich caramelized cream
crème caramel	caramel pudding
île flottante	meringues floating in cream sauce
mille feuille	light pastry (literally "1000 sheets")
mousse au chocolat	ultra-chocolate pudding
profitterolle	cream puff filled with ice cream
tarte tatin	French apple pie

Drinking

Water, milk and juice:

mineral water...	**eau minérale...**	oh mee-nay-rahl
...carbonated	**...gazeuse**	gah-zuhz
...not carbonated	**...non gazeuse**	noh<u>n</u> gah-zuhz
tap water	**l'eau du robinet**	loh dew roh-bee-nay
whole milk	**lait entier**	lay ah<u>n</u>t-yay
skim milk	**lait écrémé**	lay ay-kray-may
fresh milk	**lait frais**	lay fray
chocolate milk	**lait au chocolat**	lay oh shoh-koh-lah
hot chocolate	**chocolat chaud**	shoh-koh-lah shoh
fruit juice	**jus de fruit**	zhew duh frwee
orange juice	**jus d'orange**	zhew doh-rah<u>n</u>zh
apple juice	**jus de pomme**	zhew duh pohm
hard apple cider	**cidre**	see-druh
with / without...	**avec / sans...**	ah-vehk / sah<u>n</u>
...ice / sugar	**...glaçons / sucre**	glah-soh<u>n</u> / sew-kruh
glass / cup	**verre / tasse**	vehr / tahs
small bottle	**petite bouteille**	puh-teet boo-teh-ee
large bottle	**grande bouteille**	grah<u>n</u>d boo-teh-ee
Is the water safe to drink?	**L'eau est potable?**	loh ay poh-tah-bluh

To get free tap water at a restaurant, say, *"L'eau du robinet, s'il vous plaît."* The French typically order mineral water (and wine) with their meals. The half-liter plastic water-bottles with screw tops are light and sturdy—great to pack along and re-use as you travel.

Every *café* or *bar* has a complete price list posted. In bigger cities, prices go up when you sit down. It's cheapest to stand at the bar (*au bar* or *au comptoir*), more expensive to sit in the dining room (*la salle*) and most expensive to sit outside (*la terrasse*). Refills aren't free.

Coffee and tea:

coffee...	café...	kah-fay
...black	...noir	nwahr
...with milk	...crème	krehm
...with lots of milk	...au lait	oh lay
...American-style	...américain	ah-may-ree-kan
espresso	express	"express"
instant coffee	Nescafé	"Nescafé"
decaffeinated, decaf	décaféiné, déca	day-kah-fay-nay, day-kah
sugar	sucre	sew-kruh
hot water	l'eau chaude	loh shohd
tea / lemon	thé / citron	tay / see-trohn
tea bag	sachet de thé	sah-shay duh tay
herbal tea	tisane	tee-zahn
lemon tea, orange tea	thé au citron, thé à l'orange	tay oh see-trohn, tay ah loh-rahnzh
small / big	petit / grand	puh-tee / grahn
Another cup.	Encore une tasse.	ahn-kor ewn tahs
Is it the same price if I sit or stand?	C'est le même prix au bar ou dans la salle?	say luh mehm pree oh bar oo dahn lah sahl

In France, wine is a work of art.

Each wine-growing region and each vintage has its own distinct personality. I prefer drinking wine from the region I'm in. Ask for *vin de la région*, available at reasonable prices. To get a decent table wine in a region that doesn't produce wine (Normandy, Brittany, Paris/Île de France), ask for *un Côtes du Rhone*.

Alsace specializes in white wines: try the *Reisling, Tokay,* and *Slyvaner*.

Bordeaux offers elegant, expensive red wines, along with *Sauternes* (a sweet dessert wine) and *Graves* (a fine white).

Burgundy has the best *Chardonnay* in France. Its reds are mostly *Pinot Noir*—to save money, try a *Gamay*.

The people of **Brittany** are proud of their *Muscadet* (excellent with seafood).

In **Périgord**, try the full-bodied red *Cahors*.

The **Loire Valley** produces dry whites (*Sancerre* and *Pouilly Fumé*) and the sweet white *Vouvray* wines.

Fruity reds rule **Provence**—look for *Côtes du Rhône* and *Chateauneuf du Pape*.

Hilly **Champagne** pops the cork on the finest champagne in the world. As you explore France, look for the *dégustation* signs welcoming you in for a wine tasting. It's normally free or very cheap.

Wine:

I would like...	**Je voudrais...**	zhuh voo-dray
We would like...	**Nous voudrions...**	noo voo-dree-oh<u>n</u>
...a glass	**...un verre**	uh<u>n</u> vehr
...a carafe	**...une carafe**	ewn kah-rahf
...a half bottle	**...une demi-bouteille**	ewn duh-mee-boo-teh-ee
...a bottle	**...une bouteille**	ewn boo-teh-ee
...of red wine	**...de vin rouge**	duh va<u>n</u> roozh
...of white wine	**...de vin blanc**	duh va<u>n</u> blah<u>n</u>
...of the region	**...de la région**	duh lah ray-zhee-oh<u>n</u>
...the wine list	**...la carte des vins**	lah kart day va<u>n</u>

Wine words:

wine	**vin**	va<u>n</u>
table wine	**vin de table**	va<u>n</u> duh tah-bluh
cheapest house wine	**vin ordinaire**	va<u>n</u> or-dee-nair
local	**régional**	ray-zhee-oh-nahl
red	**rouge**	roozh
white	**blanc**	blah<u>n</u>
rosé	**rosé**	roh-zay
sparkling	**mousseux**	moo-suh
sweet	**doux**	doo
medium	**demi-sec**	duh-mee-sehk
dry	**sec**	sehk
very dry	**brut**	brewt
cork	**bouchon**	boo-shoh<u>n</u>

EATING

Beer:

beer	**bière**	bee-ehr
from the tap	**a là pression**	ah lah preh-see-oh<u>n</u>
bottle	**bouteille**	boo-teh-ee
light / dark	**blonde / brune**	bloh<u>n</u>d / brewn
local / imported	**régionale / importée**	ray-zhee-oh-nahl / a<u>n</u>-por-tay
a small beer	**un demi**	uh<u>n</u> duh-mee
a large beer	**une chope**	ewn shohp
low calorie beer (hard to find)	**biere "light"**	bee-ehr "light"
alcohol-free	**sans alcool**	sah<u>n</u>z ahl-kohl
cold / colder	**fraîche / plus fraîche**	fraysh / plew fraysh

Bar talk:

What would you like?	**Qu'est-ce que vous prenez?**	kehs kuh voo pruh-nay
What is the local specialty?	**Quelle est la spécialité régionale?**	kehl ay lah spay-see-ah-lee-tay ray-zhee-oh-nahl
Straight.	**Sec.**	sehk
With / Without...	**Avec / Sans...**	ah-vehk / sah<u>n</u>
...alcohol.	**...alcool.**	ahl-kohl
...ice.	**...glaçons.**	glah-soh<u>n</u>
One more.	**Encore une.**	ah<u>n</u>-kor ewn
Cheers!	**Santé!**	sah<u>n</u>-tay
To your health!	**À votre santé!**	ah voh-truh sah<u>n</u>-tay
Long live France!	**Vive la France!**	veev lah frah<u>n</u>s
I'm feeling...	**Je suis...**	zhuh sweez
...a little drunk.	**...un peu ivre.**	uh<u>n</u> puh ee-vruh
...blitzed. (m / f)	**...ivre mort / morte.**	ee-vruh mor / mort

An *apéritif* is served before dinner, and a *digestif* is served after dinner. Ask what's local. Typical *apéritifs* are *champagne, bière* (beer), *kir* (white wine and black currant liqueur), and *Pernod* (anise-flavored liqueur). Common *digestifs* (for after the meal) are *cognac, armagnac* (brandy), *calvados* (apple brandy), and *eaux de vie* (fruit brandy).

Picnicking

At the market:

Is it self-service?	**C'est libre service?**	say lee-bruh sehr-vees
Ripe for today?	**Pour manger aujourd'hui?**	poor mah<u>n</u>-zhay oh-joord-wee
Does it need to be cooked?	**Est'ce qu'il faut le faire cuire?**	ehs keel foh luh fehr kweer
May I taste a little?	**Je peux goûter un peu?**	zhuh puh goo-tay uh<u>n</u> puh
Fifty grams.	**Cinquante grammes.**	sa<u>n</u>-kah<u>n</u>t grahm
One hundred grams.	**Cent grammes.**	sah<u>n</u> grahm
More. / Less.	**Plus. / Moins.**	plew / mwa<u>n</u>
A piece.	**Un morceau.**	uh<u>n</u> mor-soh
A slice.	**Une tranche.**	ewn trah<u>n</u>sh
Sliced (fine).	**Tranché (fine).**	trah<u>n</u>-shay (feen)
A small bag.	**Un petit sachet.**	uh<u>n</u> puh-tee sah-shay
A bag, please.	**Un sachet, s'il vous plaît.**	uh<u>n</u> sah-shay see voo play
Can you make me a sandwich?	**Pouvez-vous me faire un sandwich?**	poo-vay-voo muh fehr uh<u>n</u> sah<u>n</u>d-weech
To take out.	**Pour emporter.**	poor ah<u>n</u>-por-tay
Is there a park nearby?	**Il y a un parc près d'ici?**	eel yah uh<u>n</u> park preh dee-see
Is it O.K. to picnic here?	**Est-ce qu'on peut pique-niquer ici?**	ehs koh<u>n</u> puh peek-nee-kay ee-see
Enjoy your meal!	**Bon appétit!**	boh<u>n</u> ah-pay-tee

Ask if there's a *marché* (open air market) nearby. These lively markets offer the best selection and ambience.

EATING

80 Eating

Picnic prose:

open air market	**marché**	mar-shay
grocery store	**épicerie**	ay-pee-suh-ree
supermarket	**supermarché**	sew-pehr-mar-shay
super-duper market	**hypermarché**	ee-pehr-mar-shay
picnic	**pique-nique**	peek-neek
sandwich	**sandwich**	sahnd-weech
(whole wheat) bread	**pain (complet)**	pan (kohn-play)
roll	**petit pain**	puh-tee pan
ham	**jambon**	zhahn-bohn
sausage	**saucisse**	soh-sees
cheese	**fromage**	froh-mahzh
mustard in a tube	**moutarde in tube**	moo-tard een tewb
mayonnaise in a tube	**mayonnaise in tube**	mah-yuh-nehz een tewb
yogurt	**yaourt**	yah-oort
fruit	**fruit**	frwee
box of juice	**boîte de jus**	bwaht duh zhew
cold drinks	**boissons fraîches**	bwah-sohn fraysh
spoon / fork...	**cuillère / fourchette...**	kwee-yehr / foor-sheht
...made of plastic	**...en plastique**	ahn plah-steek
cup / plate...	**gobelet / assiette...**	gob-leh / ahs-yeht
...made of plastic	**...en plastique**	ahn plahs-teek

While you can opt for the one-stop *supermarché*, it's more fun to visit the small shops: *boulangerie* for bread, *charcuterie* (meat), and *fromagerie* (cheese). Order meat and cheese by the gram (a hundred grams is about ¼ pound, enough for two sandwiches). At small grocery shops, clerks usually select and weigh your produce; at supermarkets, it's self-service. Watch and imitate locals. For ready-made sandwiches, try the *boulangerie* (bakery).

French-English Menu Decoder

This handy decoder won't list every word on the menu, but it'll help you get *riz et veau* (rice and veal) instead of *ris de veau* (calf pancreas).

à la carte side dishes	**boeuf** beef
abricot apricot	**boissons** beverages
agneau lamb	**bon** good
ail garlic	**bonbons** candy
aïoli garlic mayonnaise	**bouillabaisse** seafood stew
alcool alcohol	**bouilli** boiled
amande almond	**bouillon** broth
ananas pineapple	**Bourguignon** cooked in red wine
anchois anchovies	**bouteille** bottle
Anglaise boiled	**brocoli** broccoli
artichaut artichoke	**brouillés** scrambled
aspèrges asparagus	**brune** dark
assiette plate	**brut** very dry
aubergine eggplant	**cabillaud** cod
avec with	**cacahuete** peanut
baguette bread	**café** coffee
baies berries	**calmar** squid
banane banana	**canard** duck
Béarnaise sauce of egg and wine	**carafe** carafe
betterave beets	**carottes** carrots
beurre butter	**carte des vins** wine list
bière beer	**carte** menu
bifteck beef steak	**cassoulet** bean and meat stew
bisque shellfish chowder	**cerise** cherry
blanc white	**cervelle** brains
blonde light	**champignons** mushrooms

MENU DECODER

chataîgne chestnut
chaud hot
chausson fruit pastry
cheval horse
chèvre goat
chinois Chinese
chocolat chocolate
chope large beer
chou cabbage
chou-fleur cauliflower
cidre hard apple cider
citron lemon
complet whole, full
compris included
concombre cucumber
confiture jelly
consommé broth
copieux filling
coq rooster
cornichon pickle
côtelette cutlet
coupe scoop
courgette zucchini
couvert cover charge
crabe crab
crème cream
crème chantilly whipped cream
crêpe crepe
crêpes froment buckwheat crepes
crevettes shrimp
croque madame ham, cheese, & egg sandwich

croque monsieur ham & cheese sandwich
cru raw
crudités raw vegetables
cuisses de grenouilles frog legs
cuit cooked
cuit au four baked
datte date
déjeuner lunch
demi half, small beer
demi-bouteille half bottle
demi-sec medium dry
dinde turkey
dîner dinner
doux mild, sweet
eau water
entier whole
entrecôte rib steak
entrée first course
épinards spinach
escargots snails
et and
express espresso
farci stuffed
faux-filet flank steak
figue fig
filet fillet
flambée flaming
foie liver
forestière with mushrooms
frais fresh
fraise strawberry

framboise raspberry
frit fried
froid cold
fromage cheese
fruit fruit
fruits de mer seafood
fumé smoked
galette buckwheat crepe
garni with vegetables
gâteau cake
gazeuse carbonated
glace ice cream
glaçons ice
grand large
gras fat
gratinée topped with cheese
grenouille frog
grillades mixed grill
grillé grilled
gruyère Swiss cheese
hareng herring
haricots beans
hollandaise sauce of egg and
butter
homard lobster
hors-d'oeuvre appetizers
huile oil
huîtres oysters
importée imported
jambon ham
jardinière with vegetables
jus juice

lait milk
laitue lettuce
langue tongue
lapin bunny
léger light
légumes vegetables
light light
madeleine buttery cake
maïs corn
maison house
mandarine tangerine
marron chestnut
melon canteloupe
menu du jour menu of the day
meunière fried in butter
micro-ondes microwave
miel honey
mixte mixed
morceau piece
morue salty cod
moules mussels
mousseux sparkling
moutarde mustard
noir black
noisette hazelnut
noix walnut
noix de coco coconut
non not
nouvelle new
oeufs eggs
oignon onion
olives olives

onglet   steak
orange   orange
ou   or
pain   bread
pamplemousse   grapefruit
pastèque   watermelon
pâté   paté
pâtes   pasta
pâtisserie   pastry
pêche   peach
petit   small
petit déjeuner   breakfast
petits gâteaux   cookies
piquant   spicy hot
plat principal   main course
plat du jour   special of the day
plâteau   platter
poché   poached
poire   pear
poireaux   leeks
pois   peas
poisson   fish
poivre   pepper
poivron   bell pepper
pomme   apple
pomme de terre   potato
pommes frites   French fries
porc   pork
potage   soup
poulet   chicken
pour emporter   "to go"
pression   draft (beer)

prix fixe   fixed price
provençale   with garlic and tomatoes
prune   plum
pruneau   prune
ragoût   meat stew
raisins   grapes
ratatouille   eggplant casserole
régionale   local
ris de veau   sweetbreads
riz   rice
rosbif   roast beef
rosé   rosé
rôti   roasted
rouge   red
saignant   rare
salade   salad
sans   without
saucisse   sausage
saumon   salmon
scampi   prawns
sec   dry
sel   salt
service compris   service included
service non compris   service not included
sliced   tranché
sorbet   sherbet
soupe   soup
spécialité   specialty
steak tartare   raw hamburger
sucre   sugar

tartare raw
tarte pie
tartelette tart
tasse cup
terrine paté
thè tea
thon tuna
tisane herbal tea
tournedos prime cut steak
tranche slice
tripes tripe
truffes truffles (earthy mushrooms)
truite trout
vapeur steamed
variés assorted
veau veal
végétarien vegetarian
verre glass
vert green
viande meat
vin wine
vinaigre vinegar
volaille poultry
yaourt yogurt

Sightseeing

Where is...?	Où est...?	oo ay
...the best view	...la meilleure vue	lah meh-yur vew
...the main square	...la place principale	lah plahs pran-see-pahl
...the old town center	...la vieille ville	lah vee-yay-ee veel
...the museum	...le musée	luh mew-zay
...the castle	...le château	luh shah-toh
...the palace	...le palais	luh pah-lay
...the ruins	...les ruines	lay rween
...the tourist information office	...l'office du tourisme	loh-fees dew too-reez-muh
...toilet	...les toilettes	lay twah-leht
...the entrance / exit	...l'entrée / la sortie	lahn-tray / lah sor-tee
Is there a festival nearby?	Y a-t-il un festival dans la région?	eh ah-teel uhn fehs-tee-vahl dahn lah ray-zhee-ohn
Do you have...?	Avez-vous...?	ah-vay-voo
...a map	...une plan	ewn plahn
...information	...des renseigne-ments	day rahn-sehn-yuh-mahn
...a guidebook	...une guide	ewn geed
...a tour	...une visite guidée	ewn vee-zeet gee-day
...in English	...en anglais	ahn ahn-glay
When is the next tour in English?	La prochaine visite en anglais sera à quelle heure?	lah proh-shehn vee-zeet ahn ahn-glay suh-rah ah kehl ur
Is it free?	Est-ce gratuit?	ehs grah-twee
How much is it?	Combien?	kohn-bee-an

Is the ticket good all day?	Le billet est valable toute la journée?	luh bee-yay ay vah-lah-bluh toot lah zhoor-nay
Can I get back in?	Je peux rentrer?	zhuh puh rahn-tray
When does this...?	Ça... à quelle heure?	sah... ah kehl ur
...open	...ouvre	oo-vruh
...close	...ferme	fehrm
What time is the last entry?	La dernière entrée est à quelle heure?	lah dehrn-yehr ahn-tray ayt ah kehl ur
PLEASE let me in.	S'IL VOUS PLAÎT, laissez-moi entrer.	see voo play lay-say-mwah ahn-tray
I've traveled all the way from...	Je suis venu de...	zhuh swee vuh-new duh
I must leave tomorrow.	Il faut que je parte demain.	eel foh kuh zhuh part duh-man
I promise I'll be fast.	Je promets d'aller vite.	zhuh proh-may dah-lay veet

To decipher entrance signs, look for these key words: *adultes* (the price you'll pay if you're an adult), *dernière entrée* (last admission before the site closes), *exposition* (special exhibit), *ticket global* (combination ticket with another site), *visite guidée* (tour), and *vous êtes ici* (means "you are here"—you'll see it on maps).

Discounts:

You may be eligible for a discount at tourist sites, hotels, or on buses and trains—ask.

| Is there a discount for...? | Y a-t-il une réduction pour...? | ee ah-teel ewn ray-dewk-see-ohn poor |
| ...youth | ...les jeunesse | lay juh-nehs |

SIGHTSEEING

...students	...les étudiants	layz ay-tew-dee-ah<u>n</u>
...families	...les familles	lay fah-meel
...seniors	...les gens âgés	lay zhah<u>n</u> ah-zhay
I am...	J'ai...	zhay
He / She is...	Il / Elle a...	eel / ehl ah
...years old.	...___ ans.	ah<u>n</u>

In the museum:

Where is...?	Où est...?	oo ay
I'd like to see...	Je voudrais voir...	zhuh voo-dray vwahr
Photo / video O.K.?	Photo / vidéo O.K.?	foh-toh / vee-day-oh "O.K."
No flash / tripod.	Pas de flash / trépied.	pah duh flahsh / tray-pee-yay
I like it.	Ça me plaît.	sah muh play
It's so...	C'est si...	say see
...beautiful.	...belle.	behl
...ugly.	...laid.	leh
...strange.	...bizarre.	bee-zar
...boring.	...ennuyeux.	ah<u>n</u>-new-yuh
...interesting.	...intéressant.	a<u>n</u>-tay-reh-sah<u>n</u>
Wow!	Sensass!	sah<u>n</u>-sahs
My feet hurt!	J'ai mal aux pieds!	zhay mahl oh pee-yay
I'm exhausted!	Je suis épuisé!	zhuh sweez ay-pwee-zay

France's national museums close on Tuesdays. For efficient sightseeing in Paris, buy a Museum Pass. It'll save you money and time (because you're entitled to slip right into museums, bypassing the notorious lines).

Art and architecture:

art	**art**	ar
artist	**artiste**	ar-teest
painting	**tableau**	tah-bloh
self-portrait	**autoportrait**	oh-toh-por-tray
sculptor	**sculpteur**	skewlp-tur
sculpture	**sculpture**	skewlp-tewr
architect	**architecte**	ar-shee-tehkt
architecture	**architecture**	ar-shee-tehk-tewr
original	**original**	oh-ree-zhee-nahl
restored	**restauré**	rehs-toh-ray
B.C.	**av. J.-C.**	ah-vah<u>n</u> zhay-zew-kree
A.D.	**ap. J.-C.**	ah-preh zhay-zew-kree
century	**siècle**	see-eh-kluh
style	**style**	steel
Abstract	**abstrait**	ahb-stray
Ancient	**ancien**	ah<u>n</u>-see-a<u>n</u>
Art Nouveau	**art nouveau**	ar noo-voh
Baroque	**baroque**	bah-rohk
Classical	**classique**	klahs-seek
Gothic	**gothique**	goh-teek
Impressionist	**impressionniste**	a<u>n</u>-preh-see-uh-neest
Medieval	**médiéval**	mayd-yay-vahl
Modern	**moderne**	moh-dehrn
Neoclassical	**néoclassique**	nay-oh-klah-seek
Renaissance	**renaissance**	ruh-nay-sah<u>n</u>s
Romanesque	**romanesque**	roh-mah-nehsk
Romantic	**romantique**	roh-mah<u>n</u>-teek

Castles and palaces:

castle	**château**	shah-toh
fortified castle	**château-fort**	shah-toh-for
palace	**palais**	pah-lay

kitchen	**cuisine**	kwee-zeen
cellar	**cave**	kahv
castle keep	**donjon**	doh<u>n</u>-zhoh<u>n</u>
moat	**fossé**	foh-say
fortified wall	**remparts**	rah<u>n</u>-par
tower	**tour**	toor
fountain	**fontaine**	foh<u>n</u>-teh<u>n</u>
garden	**jardin**	zhar-da<u>n</u>
king	**roi**	rwah
queen	**reine**	rehn
knights	**chevaliers**	shuh-vahl-yay

Religious words:

cathedral	**cathédrale**	kah-tay-drahl
church	**église**	ay-gleez
monastery	**monastère**	moh-nah-stehr
synagogue	**synagogue**	see-nah-gohg
chapel	**chapelle**	shah-pehl
altar	**autel**	oh-tehl
cross	**croix**	krwah
cloister	**cloître**	klwah-truh
crypt	**crypte**	kreept
dome	**dôme**	dohm
bells	**cloches**	klohsh
organ	**orgue**	org
relic	**relique**	ruh-leek
saint (male / female)	**saint / sainte**	sah<u>n</u> / sah<u>nt</u>
God	**Dieu**	dee-uh
Jew	**juif**	zhweef
Moslem	**musulman**	mew-zewl-mah<u>n</u>
Christian	**chrétien**	kray-tee-a<u>n</u>
Protestant	**protestant**	proh-tehs-tah<u>n</u>

Catholic	**catholique**	kah-toh-leek
agnostic	**agnostique**	ahn-yoh-steek
atheist	**athée**	ah-tay
When is the service?	**La messe est à quelle heure?**	lah mehs ayt ah kehl ur
Are there church concerts?	**Y a-t-il des concerts à l'église?**	ee ah-teel day koh<u>n</u>-sehr ah lay-gleez

Shopping

Names of French shops:

Where is a...?	**Où est un...?**	oo ay uh<u>n</u>
antique shop	**antiquités**	ah<u>n</u>-tee-kee-tay
art gallery	**gallerie d'art**	gah-luh-ree dar
bakery	**boulangerie**	boo-lah<u>n</u>-zhuh-ree
barber shop	**coiffeur**	kwah-fur
beauty salon	**coiffeur pour dames**	kwah-fur poor dahm
book shop	**librairie**	lee-bray-ree
camera shop	**magasin de photo**	mah-gah-za<u>n</u> duh foh-toh
cheese shop	**fromagerie**	froh-mah-zhay-ree
department store	**grand magasin**	grah<u>n</u> mah-gah-za<u>n</u>
flea market	**marché aux puces**	mar-shay oh pews
flower market	**marché aux fleurs**	mar-shay oh flur
grocery store	**épicerie**	ay-pee-suh-ree
hardware store	**quincaillerie**	ka<u>n</u>-kay-yay-ree
jewelry shop	**bijouterie**	bee-zhoo-tuh-ree
laundromat	**laverie**	lah-vuh-ree

newsstand	**maison de la presse**	meh-zohn duh lah prehs
office supplies	**papeterie**	pah-pay-tuh-ree
open air market	**marché en plein air**	mar-shay ahn plan air
optician	**opticien**	ohp-tee-see-an
pharmacy	**pharmacie**	far-mah-see
photocopy shop	**magasin de photocopie**	mah-gah-zan duh foh-toh-koh-pee
shopping mall	**centre commercial**	sahn-truh koh-mehr-see-ahl
souvenir shop	**boutique de souvenirs**	boo-teek duh soo-vuh-neer
supermarket	**supermarché**	sew-pehr-mar-shay
toy store	**magasin de jouets**	mah-gah-zan duh zhway
travel agency	**agence de voyages**	ah-zhahns duh voy-yahzh
used bookstore	**boutique de livres d'occasion**	boo-teek duh lee-vruh doh-kah-zee-ohn
wine shop	**marchand de vin**	mar-shahn duh van

In France, most shops close for a long lunch (noon till about 14:00), and all day on Sundays and Mondays. Grocery stores are often open on Sunday mornings.

The French definition of customer service is different from ours. At department stores, be prepared to be treated as if you're intruding on the clerk's privacy. Exchanges are possible with receipts. Refunds are difficult. Buy to keep.

Shop till you drop:

sale	**solde**	sohld
How much is it?	**Combien?**	kohn-bee-an
I'm just browsing.	**Je regarde.**	zhuh ruh-gard

We're just browsing.	**Nous regardons.**	noo ruh-gar-doh<u>n</u>
I'd like...	**Je voudrais...**	zhuh voo-dray
Do you have...?	**Avez-vous...?**	ah-vay-voo
...something cheaper	**...quelque chose de moins cher**	kehl-kuh shohz duh mwa<u>n</u> shehr
Can I see more?	**Puis-je en voir d'autres?**	pwee zhuh ah<u>n</u> vwahr doh-truh
This one.	**Ceci.**	suh-see
Can I try it on?	**Je peux l'essayer?**	zhuh puh leh-say-yay
A mirror?	**Un miroir?**	uh<u>n</u> meer-wahr
Too...	**Trop...**	troh
...big.	**...grand.**	grah<u>n</u>
...small.	**...petit.**	puh-tee
...expensive.	**...cher.**	shehr
Did you make this?	**C'est vous qui l'avez fait?**	say voo kee lah-vay fay
What is it made out of?	**De quoi est-ce que c'est fait?**	duh kwah ehs kuh say fay
Machine washable?	**Lavable en machine?**	lah-vah-bluh ah<u>n</u> mah-sheen
Will it shrink?	**Ça va rétrécir?**	sah vah ray-tray-seer
Can you ship this?	**Pouvez-vous l'expédier?**	poo-vay-voo lehk-spay-dee-ay
Credit card O.K.?	**Carte de crédit O.K.?**	kart duh kray-dee "O.K."
Tax-free?	**Detaxé?**	day-tahks-ay
I'll think about it.	**Je vais y penser.**	zhuh vay ee pah<u>n</u>-say
What time do you close?	**Vous fermez à quelle heure?**	voo fehr-may ah kehl ur
What time do you open tomorrow?	**À quelle heure allez-vous ouvrir demain?**	ah kehl ur ah-lay-vooz oo-vreer duh-ma<u>n</u>

SHOPPING

Is that your lowest price?	C'est votre prix le plus bas?	say voh-truh pree luh plew bah
My last offer.	Ma dernière offre.	mah dehrn-yehr oh-fruh
I'm nearly broke.	Je suis presque fauché.	zhuh swee prehsk foh-shay
My friend has the money.	Mon ami a l'argent.	mohn ah-mee ah lar-zhahn
My husband...	Mon mari...	mohn mah-ree
My wife...	Ma femme...	mah fahm
...has the money.	...a l'argent.	ah lar-zhahn

You can look up colors and fabrics in the dictionary near the end of this book.

Repair:
These handy lines can apply to any repair, whether it's a stuck zipper, broken leg, or dying car.

This is broken.	C'est cassé.	say kah-say
Can you fix it?	Pouvez-vous le réparer?	poo-vay-voo luh ray-pah-ray
Just do the essentials.	Ne faites que le minimum.	nuh fayt kuh luh mee-nee-muhm
How much will it cost?	C'est combien?	say kohn-bee-an
When will it be ready?	Quand sera-t-il prêt?	kahn suh-rah-teel preh
I need it by ___.	Il me le faut pour ___.	eel muh luh foh poor

Entertainment

What's happening tonight?	**Qu'est-ce qui ce passe ce soir?**	kehs kee suh pahs suh swahr
What do you recommend?	**Qu'est-ce que vous recommandez?**	kehs kuh voo ruh-koh-mah<u>n</u>-day
Is it free?	**C'est gratuit?**	say grah-twee
Where can I buy a ticket?	**Où puis-je acheter un billet?**	oo pwee-zhuh ah-shuh-tay uh<u>n</u> bee-yay
When does it start?	**Ça commence à quelle heure?**	sah koh-mah<u>ns</u> ah kehl ur
When does it end?	**Ça se termine à quelle heure?**	sah suh tehr-meen ah kehl ur
Will you go out with me?	**Voulez-vous sortir avec moi?**	voo-lay-voo sor-teer ah-vehk mwah
The best place to dance nearby?	**Le meilleur dancing dans le coin?**	luh meh-yur dah<u>n</u>-seeng dah<u>n</u> luh kwa<u>n</u>
Do you want to dance?	**Voulez-vous danser?**	voo-lay-voo dah<u>n</u>-say
Again?	**De nouveau?**	duh noo-voh
Let's celebrate!	**Faisons la fête!**	fay-zoh<u>n</u> lah feht
Let's have fun like idiots.	**Amusons-nous comme des fous.**	ah-mew-zoh<u>n</u>-noo kohm day foo

Cafes, very much a part of the French social scene, are places for friends to spend the evening together. To meet new friends, the French look for *pubs* or *bars américains*.

ENTERTAINMENT

Entertaining words:

movie...	**film...**	feelm
...original version	**...version** **originale (V.O.)**	vehr-see-oh<u>n</u> oh-ree-zhee-nahl
...in English	**...en anglais**	ah<u>n</u> ah<u>n</u>-glay
...with subtitles	**...avec sous-titres**	ah-vehk soo-tee-truh
...dubbed	**...doublé**	doo-blay
music...	**musique...**	mew-zeek
...live	**...en directe**	ah<u>n</u> dee-rehkt
...classical	**...classique**	klahs-seek
...folk	**...folklorique**	fohk-loh-reek
old rock	**rock classique**	rohk klah-seek
jazz	**jazz**	zhazz
blues	**blues**	"blues"
male singer	**chanteur**	shah<u>n</u>-tur
female singer	**chanteuse**	shah<u>n</u>-tuhz
nightclub	**boite**	bwaht
concert	**concert**	koh<u>n</u>-sehr
show	**spectacle**	spehk-tahk-luh
sound and light show	**son et lumière**	soh<u>n</u> ay lew-mee-ehr
dancing	**danse**	dah<u>n</u>s
folk dancing	**danse folklorique**	dah<u>n</u>s fohk-loh-reek
disco	**disco**	dee-skoh
cover charge	**couvert**	koo-vehr

For concerts and special events, ask at the local tourist office.

Paris has a great cinema scene, especially on the Champs-Élysées. Pick up a *Pariscope*, the periodical entertainment guide, and choose from hundreds of films (often discounted on Mondays). Those listed V.O. (rather than V.F.) are in their original language.

Phoning

The nearest phone?	**Le plus proche téléphone?**	luh plew prohsh tay-lay-fohn
Where's the post office?	**Où est la Poste?**	oo ay lah pohst
I'd like to telephone...	**Je voudrais téléphoner...**	zhuh voo-dray tay-lay-foh-nay
...the U.S.A.	**...aux U.S.A.**	ohz ew ehs ah
What is the cost per minute?	**C'est combien par minute?**	say kohn-bee-an par mee-newt
I'd like to make a... call.	**Je voudrais faire un appel...**	zhuh voo-dray fair uhn ah-pehl
...local	**...local.**	loh-kahl
...collect	**...en P.C.V.**	ahn pay say vay
...credit card	**...avec une carte de crédit.**	ah-vehk ewn kart duh kray-dee
...long distance (within France)	**...interurbain.**	an-tehr-ewr-ban
...international	**...international.**	an-tehr-nah-see-oh-nahl
It doesn't work.	**Ça ne marche pas.**	sah nuh marsh pah
May I use your phone?	**Puis-je téléphoner?**	pwee-zhuh tay-lay-foh-nay
Can you dial for me?	**Pouvez-vous composer le numéro?**	poo-vay-voo kohn-poh-zay luh new-may-roh
Can you talk for me?	**Pouvez-vous parler pour moi?**	poo-vay-voo par-lay poor mwah
It's busy.	**C'est occupé.**	say oh-kew-pay
Will you try again?	**Essayez de nouveau?**	eh-say-yay duh noo-voh
Hello. (on the phone)	**Âllo.**	ah-loh
My name is...	**Je m'appelle...**	zhuh mah-pehl

PHONING, E-MAIL

My number is...	**Mon numéro est...**	mohn new-may-roh ay
Speak slowly and clearly.	**Parlez lentement et clairement.**	par-lay lahn-tuh-mahn ay klair-mahn
Wait a moment.	**Un moment.**	uhn moh-mahn
Don't hang up.	**Ne racrochez pas.**	nuh rah-kroh-shay pah

Key telephone words:

telephone	**téléphone**	tay-lay-fohn
telephone card	**télécarte**	tay-lay-kart
post office	**Poste**	pohst
operator	**standardiste**	stahn-dar-deest
international assistance	**renseignements internationaux**	rahn-sehn-yuh-mahn an-tehr-nah-see-oh-noh
country code	**code international**	kohd an-tehr-nah-see-oh-nahl
area code	**code régional**	kohd ray-zhee-oh-nahl
telephone book	**bottin, annuaire**	boh-tan, ahn-new-air
yellow pages	**pages jaunes**	pahzh zhohn
toll-free	**gratuit**	grah-twee
out of service	**hors service**	or sehr-vees

French post offices often have metered phones. It's also easy to make a call with a handy phone card (*télécarte*), available at post offices, train stations and *tabac* (tobacco) shops. Insert the card into a phone and call anywhere in the world.

You can also buy postage stamps at *tabac* shops -- very handy, so long as you know in advance the amount of postage you need.)

E-mail

e-mail	**e-mail**	ee-mayl
internet	**internet**	an-tehr-neht
May I check my e-mail?	**Puis-je vérifier mon e-mail?**	pwee-zhuh vay-ree-fee-ay mohn ee-mayl
Where can I get access to the internet?	**Où est-ce que je peux accéder à l'internet?**	oo ehs kuh zhuh puh ahk-say-day ah lan-tehr-neht
Where is the nearest cybercafé?	**Où se trouve le cybercafé le plus prôche?**	oo suh troov luh see-behr-kah-fay luh plew prohsh

On the computer screen:

annuler	delete	**message**	message
envoyer	send	**sauver**	save
fichier	file	**ouvrir**	open
imprimer	print		

Post Office

Where is the post office?	**Où est la Poste?**	oo ay luh pohst
Which window for...?	**Quel guichet pour...?**	kehl gee-shay poor
...stamps	**...les timbres**	lay tan-bruh
...packages	**...les colis**	lay koh-lee
To the United States...	**Aux Etats-Unis...**	ohz ay-tah-zew-nee
...by air mail.	**...par avion.**	par ah-vee-ohn
...by surface mail.	**...par surface.**	par sewr-fahs
How much is it?	**Combien?**	kohn-bee-an

E-MAIL, POST

How many days will it take?	**Ça va prendre combien de jours?**	sah vah prah<u>n</u>-druh koh<u>n</u>-bee-a<u>n</u> duh zhoor

Licking the postal code:

post office	**La Poste**	lah pohst
stamp	**timbre**	ta<u>n</u>-bruh
postcard	**carte postale**	kart poh-stahl
letter	**lettre**	leht-ruh
aerogram	**aérogramme**	ay-roh-grahm
envelope	**enveloppe**	ah<u>n</u>-vuh-lohp
package	**colis**	koh-lee
box	**boîte en carton**	bwaht ah<u>n</u> kar-toh<u>n</u>
string / tape	**ficelle / scotch**	fee-sehl / skotch
mailbox	**boîte aux lettres**	bwaht oh leht-truh
air mail	**par avion**	par ah-vee-oh<u>n</u>
express	**par express**	par ehk-sprehs
surface (slow & cheap)	**surface**	sewr-fahs
book rate	**tarif des livres**	tah-reef day lee-vruh
weight limit	**poids limite**	pwah lee-meet
registered	**enregistré**	ah<u>n</u>-ruh-zhee-stray
insured	**assuré**	ah-sew-ray
fragile	**fragile**	frah-zheel
contents	**contenu**	koh<u>n</u>-tuh-new
customs	**douane**	doo-ahn
to / from	**à / de**	ah / duh
address	**adresse**	ah-drehs
zip code	**code postal**	kohd poh-stahl
general delivery	**poste restante**	pohst rehs-tah<u>n</u>t

Red Tape & Profanity

Filling out forms:

Monsieur	Mr.
Madame / Mademoiselle	Mrs. / Miss
prénom	first name
nom	name
adresse	address
lieu de domicile	address
rue	street
ville	city
état	state
pays	country
nationalité	nationality
originaire de...	origin
destination	destination
âge	age
date de naissance	date of birth
lieu de naissance	place of birth
sexe	sex
mâle / femelle	male / female
marié / célibataire	married / single
profession	profession
adulte	adult
enfant / garçon / fille	child / boy / girl
enfants	children
famille	family
signature	signature

RED TAPE

When filling out dates, use this order: day/month/year (Christmas is 25/12/01).

French profanity:

In any country, red tape inspires profanity. In case you're wondering what the more colorful locals are saying...

Damn! (Good God!)	**Bon Dieu!**	bohn dee-uh
bastard	**salaud**	sah-loh
bitch	**salope**	sah-lohp
breasts (colloq.)	**tétons**	tay-tohn
big breasts	**grands tétons**	grahn tay-tohn
penis (colloq.)	**bite**	beet
butthole	**sale con**	sahl kohn
shit	**merde**	mehrd
drunk	**bourré**	boo-ray
idiot	**idiot**	ee-dee-oh
imbecile	**imbécile**	an-bay-seel
jerk	**connard**	kuh-nar
stupid	**stupide**	stew-peed
Did someone...?	**Est-ce que quelqu'un à...?**	ehs kuh kehl-kuhn ah
...fart	**...péter**	pay-tay
...burp	**...roter**	roh-tay

Help!

Help!	**Au secours!**	oh suh-koor
Help me!	**A l'aide!**	ah layd
Call a doctor!	**Appelez un docteur!**	ah-play uhn dohk-tur
ambulance	**ambulance**	ahn-bew-lahns
accident	**accident**	ahk-see-dahn
injured	**blessé**	bleh-say
emergency	**urgence**	ewr-zhahns
fire	**feu**	fuh
police	**police**	poh-lees
thief	**voleur**	voh-lur
pick-pocket	**pickpocket**	peek-poh-keht
I've been ripped off.	**On m'a volé.**	ohn mah voh-lay
I've lost...	**J'ai perdu...**	zhay pehr-dew
...my passport.	**...mon passeport.**	mohn pah-spor
...my ticket.	**...mon billet.**	mohn bee-yay
...my baggage.	**...mes bagages.**	may bah-gahzh
...my purse.	**...mon sac.**	mohn sahk
...my wallet.	**...mon portefeuille.**	mohn por-tuh-fuh-ee
...my faith in humankind.	**...ma foi en l'humanité.**	mah fwah ahn lew-mah-nee-tay
I'm lost.	**Je suis perdu.**	zhuh swee pehr-dew

France's medical emergency phone number is 15. *SOS médecins* are doctors who make emergency house-calls. If you need help, someone will call an *SOS médicin* for you.

HELP!

Help for women:

Leave me alone.	**Laissez-moi tranquille.**	lay-say-mwah trah<u>n</u>-keel
I *want* to be alone.	**Je veux être seule.**	zhuh vuh eh-truh suhl
I'm not interested.	**Ça ne m'intéresse pas.**	sah nuh ma<u>n</u>-tay-rehs pah
I'm married.	**Je suis mariée.**	zhuh swee mah-ree-ay
I'm a lesbian.	**Je suis lesbienne.**	zhuh swee lehz-bee-ehn
I have a contagious disease.	**J'ai une maladie contagieuse.**	zhay ewn mah-lah-dee koh<u>n</u>-tah-zhuhz
Don't touch me.	**Ne me touchez pas.**	nuh muh too-shay pah
You're disgusting.	**Vous êtes dégoutant.**	vooz eht day-goo-tah<u>n</u>
Stop following me.	**Arrêtez de me suivre.**	ah-reh-tay duh muh swee-vruh
This man is bothering me.	**Cet homme m'embête.**	seht ohm mah<u>n</u>-beht
Enough!	**Ça suffit!**	sah sew-fee
Get lost!	**Dégagez!**	day-gah-zhay
Drop dead!	**Fous-moi la paix!**	foo-mwah lah pay
I'll call the police.	**J'appelle la police.**	zhah-pehl lah poh-lees

Health

I feel sick.	Je me sens malade.	zhuh muh sah<u>n</u> mah-lahd
I need a doctor...	Il me faut un docteur...	eel muh foh uh<u>n</u> dohk-tur
...who speaks English.	...qui parle anglais.	kee parl ah<u>n</u>-glay
It hurts here.	Ça me fait mal ici.	sah muh fay mahl ee-see
I'm allergic to...	Je suis allergique à...	zhuh sweez ah-lehr-zheek ah
...penicillin.	...la pénicilline.	lah pay-nee-see-leen
I am diabetic.	Je suis diabétique.	zhuh swee dee-ah-bay-teek
I've missed a period.	J'ai du retard dans mes règles.	zhay dew ruh-tar dah<u>n</u> may reh-gluh
My friend has...	Mon ami a...	moh<u>n</u> ah-mee ah
I have...	J'ai...	zhay
...asthma.	...asthme.	ahz-muh
...a burn.	...une brûlure.	ewn brew-lewr
...chest pains.	...mal à la poitrine.	mahl ah lah pwah-treen
...a cold.	...un rhume.	uh<u>n</u> rewm
...constipation.	...la constipation.	lah koh<u>n</u>-stee-pah-see-oh<u>n</u>
...a cough.	...une toux.	ewn too
...diarrhea.	...la diarrhée.	lah dee-ah-ray
...dizziness.	...le vertige.	luh vehr-teezh
...a fever.	...une fièvre.	ewn fee-eh-vruh
...the flu.	...la grippe.	lah greep
...the giggles.	...le fou rire.	luh foo reer
...hay fever.	...le rhume des foins.	luh rewm day fwa<u>n</u>
...a headache.	...mal à la tête.	mahl ah lah teht
...hemorrhoids.	...hémorroïdes.	ay-mor-wahd

HEALTH

...high blood pressure.	...de l'hypertension.	duh lee-pehr-tah<u>n</u>-see-oh<u>n</u>
...indigestion.	...une indigestion.	ewn a<u>n</u>-dee-zhuh-stee-oh<u>n</u>
...an infection.	...une infection.	ewn a<u>n</u>-fehk-see-oh<u>n</u>
...a migraine.	...une migraine.	ewn mee-grayn
...nausea.	...la nausée.	lah noh-zay
...a rash.	...des boutons.	day boo-toh<u>n</u>
...a sore throat.	...mal à la gorge.	mahl ah lah gorzh
...a stomach ache.	...mal à l'estomac.	mahl ah luh-stoh-mah
...a swelling.	...une enflure.	ewn ah<u>n</u>-flewr
...a toothache.	...mal aux dents.	mahl oh dah<u>n</u>
...a urinary infection.	...une infection urinarire.	ewn a<u>n</u>-fehk-see-oh<u>n</u> ew-ree-nehr
...a venereal disease.	...une maladie vénérienne.	ewn mah-lah-dee vay-nay-ree-ehn
...worms.	...des vers.	day vehr
I have body odor.	Je sens mauvais.	zhuh sah<u>n</u> moh-vay
Is it serious?	C'est sérieux?	say say-ree-uh

Handy health words:

pain	douleur	doo-lur
dentist	dentiste	dah<u>n</u>-teest
doctor	docteur	dohk-tur
nurse	garde-malade	gard-mah-lahd
health insurance	assurance maladie	ah-sew-rah<u>n</u>s mah-lah-dee
hospital	hôpital	oh-pee-tahl
bandage	bandage	bah<u>n</u>-dahzh
medicine	médicaments	may-dee-kah-mah<u>n</u>
pharmacy	pharmacie	far-mah-see
prescription	ordonnance	or-duh-nah<u>n</u>s
pill	pilule	pee-lewl

aspirin	**aspirine**	ah-spee-reen
non-aspirin substitute	**Tylenol**	tee-luh-nohl
antibiotic	**antibiotique**	ah<u>n</u>-tee-bee-oh-teek
cold medicine	**remède contre le rhume**	ruh-mehd koh<u>n</u>-truh luh rewm
cough drops	**pastilles pour la toux**	pah-steel poor lah too
pain killer	**calmant**	kahl-mah<u>n</u>
vitamins	**vitamines**	vee-tah-meen

Contacts and glasses:

glasses	**lunettes**	lew-neht
sunglasses	**lunettes de soleil**	lew-neht duh soh-lay
prescription	**ordonnance**	or-duh-nah<u>n</u>s
lenses...	**verres de...**	vehr duh
...soft / hard	**...souples / durs**	soop-luh / dewr
cleaning solution	**solution nettoyante**	soh-lew-see-oh<u>n</u> neh-toy-yah<u>n</u>t
soaking solution	**solution à trempage**	soh-lew-see-oh<u>n</u> ah trah<u>n</u>-pahzh
I've... a contact lens.	**J'ai... un de mes verres de contact.**	zhay... uh<u>n</u> duh may vehr duh koh<u>n</u>-tahkt
...lost	**...perdu**	pehr-dew
...swallowed	**...avalé**	ah-vah-lay

Toiletries:

comb	**peigne**	pehn-yuh
conditioner	**après-shampoing**	ah-preh-shah<u>n</u>-pwa<u>n</u>
condoms	**préservatifs**	pray-zehr-vah-teef
dental floss	**fil dentaire**	feel dah<u>n</u>-tair
deodorant	**déodorant**	day-oh-doh-rah<u>n</u>

hairbrush	**brosse**	brohs
hand lotion	**crème pour les mains**	krehm poor lay ma<u>n</u>
lip salve	**beaume pour les lèvres**	bohm poor lay leh-vruh
nail clipper	**pince à ongles**	pa<u>ns</u> ah oh<u>n</u>-gluh
razor	**rasoir**	rah-zwahr
sanitary napkins	**serviettes hygiéniques**	sehrv-yeht ee-zhay-neek
shampoo	**shampoing**	shah<u>n</u>-pwa<u>n</u>
shaving cream	**mousse à raser**	moos ah rah-zehr
soap	**savon**	sah-voh<u>n</u>
sunscreen	**huile solaire**	weel soh-lair
tampons	**tampons**	tah<u>n</u>-poh<u>n</u>
tissues	**mouchoirs en papier**	moosh-wahr ah<u>n</u> pah-peer
toilet paper	**papier hygiénique**	pah-peer ee-zhay-neek
toothbrush	**brosse à dents**	brohs ah dah<u>n</u>
toothpaste	**dentifrice**	dah<u>n</u>-tee-frees
tweezers	**pince à épiler**	pa<u>ns</u> ah ay-pee-lay

Chatting

My name is...	**Je m'appelle...**	zhuh mah-pehl
What's your name?	**Quel est votre nom?**	kehl ay voh-truh noh<u>n</u>
How are you?	**Comment allez-vous?**	koh-mah<u>n</u>t ah-lay-voo
Very well, thank you.	**Très bien, merci.**	treh bee-a<u>n</u> mehr-see
Where are you from?	**D'où venez-vous?**	doo vuh-nay-voo
What city?	**Quelle ville?**	kehl veel
What country?	**Quel pays?**	kehl pay-ee
What planet?	**Quelle planète?**	kehl plah-neht
I am...	**Je suis...**	zhuh swee
...a male American.	**...américain.**	zah-may-ree-ka<u>n</u>
...a female American.	**...américaine.**	zah-may-ree-kehn
...a male Canadian.	**...canadien.**	kah-nah-dee-a<u>n</u>
...a female Canadian.	**...canadienne.**	kah-nah-dee-ehn

Nothing more than feelings:

I am / You are...	**Je suis / Vous êtes...**	zhuh swee / vooz eht
...happy. (m / f)	**...content / contente.**	koh<u>n</u>-tah<u>n</u> / koh<u>n</u>-tah<u>n</u>t
...sad.	**...triste.**	treest
...tired.	**...fatigué.**	fah-tee-gay
I am / You are...	**J'ai / Vous avez...**	zhay / vooz ah-vay
...hungry.	**...faim.**	fa<u>n</u>
...thirsty.	**...soif.**	swahf
...homesick.	**...le mal du pays.**	luh mahl dew pay-ee
...cold.	**...froid.**	frwah
...too warm.	**...trop chaud.**	troh shoh
...lucky.	**...de la chance.**	duh lah shah<u>n</u>s

CHATTING

Who's who:

This is my friend.	**C'est mon ami.**	say mohn ah-mee
This is my... (m / f)	**C'est mon / ma...**	say mohn / mah
...boyfriend / girlfriend.	**...petit ami / petite amie.**	puh-teet ah-mee / puh-teet ah-mee
...husband / wife.	**...mari / femme.**	mah-ree / fahm
...son / daughter.	**...fils / fille.**	fees / fee-ee
...brother / sister.	**...frère / soeur.**	frehr / sur
...father / mother.	**...père / mère.**	pehr / mehr
...uncle / aunt.	**...oncle / tante.**	ohn-kluh / tahnt
...nephew / niece.	**...neveu / nièce.**	nuh-vuh / nees
...male / female cousin.	**...cousin / cousine.**	koo-zan / koo-zeen
...grandfather / grandmother.	**...grand-père / grand-mère.**	grahn-pehr / grahn-mehr
...grandson / granddaughter.	**...petit-fils / petite-fille.**	puh-tee-fees / puh-teet-feel

Family and work:

Are you married?	**Êtes-vous marié?**	eht voo mah-ree-ay
Do you have children?	**Avez-vous des enfants?**	ah-vay-voo dayz ahn-fahn
How many boys / girls?	**Combien de garçons / filles?**	kohn-bee-an duh gar-sohn / feel
Do you have photos?	**Avez-vous des photos?**	ah-vay-voo day foh-toh
How old is your child?	**Quel âge à votre enfant?**	kehl ahzh ah voh-truh ahn-fahn
Beautiful child!	**Bel enfant!**	behl ahn-fahn
Beautiful children!	**Beaux enfants!**	bohz ahn-fahn

What is your occupation?	**Quelle est votre metier?**	kehl eh voh-truh may-tee-yay
Do you like your work?	**Aimez-vous votre metier?**	eh-may-voo voh-truh may-tee-yay
I'm a...	**Je suis...**	zhuh swee
...male student.	**...étudiant.**	zay-tew-dee-ah<u>n</u>
...female student.	**...étudiante.**	zay-tew-dee-ah<u>n</u>t
...teacher.	**...professeur.**	proh-feh-sur
...worker.	**...ouvrier.**	zoo-vree-ay
...bureaucrat.	**...fonctionnaire.**	foh<u>n</u>-see-oh<u>n</u>-nair
...professional traveler.	**...voyageur professionnel.**	voy-yah-zhur proh-feh-see-oh-nehl
Can I take a photo of you?	**Puis-je prendre une photo de vous?**	pwee-zhuh prah<u>n</u>-druh ewn foh-toh duh voo

Chatting with children:

What's your first name?	**Quel est ton prénom?**	kehl ay toh<u>n</u> pray-noh<u>n</u>
My name is...	**Je m'appelle...**	zhuh mah-pehl
How old are you?	**Quel âge as-tu?**	kehl ahzh ah-tew
Do you have brothers and sisters?	**As-tu des frères et soeurs?**	ah-tew day frehr ay sur
Do you like school?	**Tu aimes l'école?**	too ehm lay-kohl
What are you studying?	**Qu'est-ce que tu étudies?**	kehs kuh tew ay-tew-dee
I'm studying...	**J'étudie...**	zhay-too-dee
What's your favorite subject?	**Quel est ton sujet préferé?**	kehl ay toh<u>n</u> soo-zhay pray-fuh-ray
Do you have pets?	**As-tu un animal chez toi?**	ah-tew uh<u>n</u> ah-nee-mahl shay twah

...cat / dog / fish	...chat / chien / poisson	shah / shee-a<u>n</u> / pwah-soh<u>n</u>
I have a...	J'ai un...	zhay uh<u>n</u>
Will you teach me some French words?	Peux-tu m'apprendre quelques mots en français?	pwuh-tew mah-prah<u>n</u>-druh kehl-kuh moh ah<u>n</u> frah<u>n</u>-say
What is this?	Qu'est-ce que c'est?	kes kuh say
Will you teach me a simple French song?	Peux-tu m'apprendre une chanson française facile?	pwuh-tew mah-prah<u>n</u>-druh ewn shah<u>n</u>-soh<u>n</u> frah<u>n</u>-sehz fah-seel
Guess which country I live in.	Devine mon pays.	duh-veen moh<u>n</u> pay-ee
How old am I?	J'ai quel âge?	zhay kehl ahzh
I'm ___ years old.	J'ai ___ ans.	zhay ___ ah<u>n</u>
Teach me a fun game.	Apprends-moi un jeu rigolo.	ah-prah<u>n</u>-mwah uh<u>n</u> zhuh ree-goh-loh
Got any candy?	As-tu des bon-bons?	ah-tew day boh<u>n</u>-boh<u>n</u>

Travel talk:

I am / Are you...?	Je suis / Êtes-vous...?	zhuh sweez / eht-vooz
...on vacation	...en vacances	ah<u>n</u> vah-kah<u>n</u>s
...on business	...en voyage d'affaires	ah<u>n</u> voy-yahzh dah-fair
How long have you been traveling?	Il y a longtemps que vous voyagez?	eel yah loh<u>n</u>-tah<u>n</u> kuh voo voy-yah-zhay
day / week	jour / semaine	zhoor / suh-mehn
month / year	mois / année	mwah / ah-nay
When are you going home?	Quand allez-vous rentrer?	kah<u>n</u> ah-lay-voo rah<u>n</u>-tray

This is my first time in...	C'est la première fois que je visite...	say lah pruhm-yehr fwah kuh zhuh vee-zeet
It's / It's not a tourist trap.	C'est / Ce n'est pas un piège à touristes.	say / suh nay pah uhn pee-ehzh ah too-reest
Today / Tomorrow I go to...	Aujourd'hui / Demain je vais à...	oh-zhoor-dwee / duh-man zhuh vay ah
I'm happy here.	Je suis content / contente ici.	zhuh swee kohn-tahn / kohn-tahnt ee-see
The French are very friendly.	Les Français sont très gentils.	lay frahn-say sohn treh zhahn-tee
France is wonderful.	La France est magnifique.	lah frahns ay mahn-yee-feek
To travel is to live.	Voyager c'est vivre.	voy-yah-zhay say vee-vruh
Have a good trip!	Bon voyage!	bohn voy-yahzh

Weather:

What's the weather tomorrow?	Quel temps fera-t-il demain?	kehl tahn fuh-rah-teel duh-man
sunny / cloudy	ensoleillé / nuageux	ahn-soh-lay-yay / nwah-zhuh
hot / cold	chaud / froid	shoh / frwah
muggy / windy	humide / venteux	oo-meed / vahn-tuh
rain / snow	pluie / neige	ploo-ee / nehzh
It's raining like a cow's piss. (French saying)	Ça pleut comme vâche qui pisse.	sah pluh kohm vahsh kee pees

CHATTING

Map talk:
Use the following maps to delve into family history.

I live here.	**J'habite ici.**	zhah-beet ee-see
I was born here.	**Je suis né là.**	zhuh swee nay lah
My ancestors came from...	**Mes ancêtres viennent de...**	mayz ah<u>n</u>-seh-truh vee-ehn duh
I've traveled to...	**J'ai visité...**	zhay vee-zee-tay
Next I'll go to...	**Et puis je vais à...**	ay pwee zhuh vay ah
Where do you live?	**Où est-ce que vous vivez?**	oo ehs kuh voo vee-vay
Where were you born?	**Où êtes-vous né?**	oo eht-voo nay
Where did your ancestors come from?	**D'où viennent vos ancêtres?**	doo vee-ehn vohz ah<u>n</u>-seh-truh
Where have you traveled?	**Où êtes-vous voyagé?**	oo eht-vooz voy-yah-zhay
Where are you going?	**Où allez-vous?**	oo ah-lay-voo
Where would you like to go?	**Où voudriez voyager?**	oo voo-dree-yay voy-yay-zhay

France

Favorite things:

What kind...	Quelle sorte...	kehl sort...
do you like?	aimez-vous?	eh-may-voo
...of art	...d'art	dar
...of books	...de livres	duh lee-vruh
...of hobby	...de hobby	duh oh-bee
...of ice cream	...de glace	duh glahs
...of movies	...de films	duh feelm
...of music	...de musique	duh mew-zeek
...of sports	...de sports	duh spor
...of vices	...de vices	duh vees
Who is your...?	Qui est votre...?	kee ay voh-truh
...favorite male singer	...chanteur favorit	shahn-tur fah-voh-ree
...favorite female singer	...chanteuse favorite	shahn-tuhz fah-voh-reet
...favorite movie star	...vedette favorite	vuh-deht fah-voh-reet

Responses for all occasions:

I like that.	Ça me plaît.	sah muh play
I like you.	Je t'aime bien.	zhuh tehm bee-an
That's cool.	C'est chouette.	say shweht
Great!	Formidable!	for-mee-dah-bluh
Perfect.	Parfait.	par-fay
Funny.	Amusant.	ah-mew-zahn
Interesting.	Intéressant.	an-tay-reh-sahn
I don't smoke.	Je ne fume pas.	zhuh nuh fewm pah
Really?	Vraiment?	vray-mahn
Congratulations!	Félicitations!	fay-lee-see-tah-see-ohn

CHATTING

Well done!	Bien joué!	bee-an zhoo-ay
You're welcome.	Je vous en prie.	zhuh vooz ahn pree
It's nothing.	De rien.	duh ree-an
Bless you! (after sneeze)	À vos souhaits!	ah voh sway
Excuse me.	Pardon.	par-dohn
What a pity.	Quel dommage.	kehl doh-mahzh
That's life.	C'est la vie.	say lah vee
No problem.	Pas de problème.	pah duh proh-blehm
O.K.	D'accord.	dah-kor
This is the good life!	Que la vie est belle!	kuh lah vee ay behl
Have a good day!	Bonne journée!	buhn zhoor-nay
Good luck!	Bonne chance!	buhn shahns
Let's go!	Allons-y!	ah-lohn-zee

Thanks a million:

Thank you very much.	Merci beaucoup.	mehr-see boh-koo
You are...	Vous êtes...	vooz eht
...helpful.	...serviable.	sehr-vee-ah-bluh
...generous.	...généreux / généreuse.	zhay-nay-ruh / zhay-nay-ruhz
It's / You are...	C'est / Vous êtes...	say / vooz eht
...wonderful.	...magnifique.	mahn-yee-feek
...great fun.	...très amusant.	trehz ah-mew-zahn
You've gone to much trouble.	Vous avez trop fait pour moi.	vooz ah-vay troh fay poor mwah
You are an angel from God.	Vous êtes un ange de Dieu.	vooz eht uhn ahnzh duh dee-uh

You spoil me / us.	**Vous me / nous gâtez.**	voo muh / noo gah-tay
I will remember you...	**Je me souviendrai...**	zhuh muh soov-yan-dreh
...always.	**...toujours.**	too-zhoor
...till Tuesday.	**...jusqu'à mardi.**	zhews-kah mar-dee

Conversing with French animals:

rooster / cock-a-doodle-doo	**coq / cocorico**	kohk / koh-koh-ree-koh
bird / tweet tweet	**oiseau / cui cui**	wah-zoh / kwee kwee
cat / meow	**chat / miaou**	shah / mee-ah-oo
dog / woof woof	**chien / ouah ouah**	shee-an / wah wah
duck / quack quack	**canard / coin coin**	kah-nar / kwan kwan
cow / moo	**vache / meu**	vahsh / muh
pig / oink oink	**cochon / groin groin**	koh-shohn / grwan grwan

Create your own conversation

The French enjoy good conversations. Join in! Using these lists, you can build sentences that will sound either deep or ridiculous, depending on your mood (and theirs).

Who:

I / you	**je / vous**	zhuh / voo
he / she	**il / elle**	eel / ehl
we / they	**nous / ils**	noo / eel
my / your...	**mes / vos...**	may / voh
...parents / children	**...parents / enfants**	pah-rahn / zahn-fahn
men / women	**hommes / femmes**	ohm / fahm
rich / poor	**riches / pauvres**	reesh / poh-vruh

politicians	**politiciens**	poh-lee-tee-see-a<u>n</u>
big business	**grosses affaires**	grohs ah-fair
mafia	**mafia**	mah-fee-ah
military	**militaire**	mee-lee-tair
the French	**les Francais**	lay frah<u>n</u>-say
the Germans	**les Allemands**	layz ahl-mah<u>n</u>
the Italians	**les Italiens**	layz ee-tah-lee-a<u>n</u>
the Americans	**les Américains**	layz ah-may-ree-ka<u>n</u>
liberals	**libéraux**	lee-bay-roh
conservatives	**conservateurs**	koh<u>n</u>-sehr-vah-tur
radicals	**radicaux**	rah-dee-koh
travelers	**voyageurs**	voy-yah-zhur
everyone	**tout le monde**	too luh moh<u>n</u>d
God	**Dieu**	dee-uh"

What:

want	**vouloir**	vool-wahr
need	**avoir besoin de**	ahv-wahr buh-swa<u>n</u> duh
take / give	**prendre / donner**	prah<u>n</u>-druh / duh-nay
love / hate	**aimer / détester**	eh-may / day-tehs-tay
work / play	**travailler / jouer**	trah-vah-yay / zhoo-way
have / lack	**avoir / manquer de**	ahv-wahr / mah<u>n</u>-kay duh
learn / fear	**apprendre / craindre**	ah-prah<u>n</u>-druh / cra<u>n</u>-druh
help / abuse	**aider / abuser**	ay-day / ah-boo-zay
prosper / suffer	**prospérer / souffrir**	proh-spay-ray / soo-freer
buy / sell	**acheter / vendre**	ah-shuh-tay / vah<u>n</u>-druh

Why:

love	**amour**	ah-moor
sex	**sexe**	"sex"
money	**argent**	ar-zhah<u>n</u>
power	**pouvoir**	poov-wahr
work	**travail**	trah-vah-ee

food	**nourriture**	noo-ree-tewr
family	**famille**	fah-mee-ee
health	**santé**	sah<u>n</u>-tay
hope	**espoir**	ehs-pwahr
education	**éducation**	ay-dew-kah-see-oh<u>n</u>
guns	**armes**	arm
religion	**religion**	ruh-lee-zhee-oh<u>n</u>
happiness	**bonheur**	boh<u>n</u>-ur
marijuana	**marijuana**	mah-ree-wah-nah
democracy	**démocratie**	day-moh-krah-see
taxes	**taxes**	tahx
lies	**mensonges**	mah<u>n</u>-soh<u>n</u>zh
corruption	**corruption**	koh-rewp-see-oh<u>n</u>
pollution	**pollution**	poh-lew-see-oh<u>n</u>
television	**télévision**	tay-lay-vee-zee-oh<u>n</u>
relaxation	**relaxation**	ruh-lahk-sah-see-oh<u>n</u>
violence	**violence**	vee-oh-lah<u>n</u>s
respect	**respect**	ruh-speh
racism	**racisme**	rah-seez-muh
war / peace	**guerre / paix**	gehr / peh
global perspective	**point de vue global**	pwa<u>n</u> duh vew gloh-bahl

You be the judge:

(no) problem	**(pas de) problème**	(pah duh) proh-blehm
(not) good	**(pas) bon**	(pah) boh<u>n</u>
(not) dangerous	**(pas) dangereux**	(pah) dah<u>n</u>-zhay-ruh
(not) fair	**(pas) juste**	(pah) zhewst
(not) guilty	**(pas) coupable**	(pah) koo-pah-bluh
(not) powerful	**(pas) fort**	(pah) for
(not) stupid	**(pas) stupide**	(pah) stew-peed
(not) happy	**(pas) content**	(pah) koh<u>n</u>-tah<u>n</u>
because / for	**parce que / pour**	pars kuh / poor
and / or / from	**et / ou / de**	ay / oo / duh
too much	**trop**	troh
enough	**assez**	ah-say

CHATTING

never enough	**jamais assez**	jah-may ah-say
worse	**pire**	peer
same	**même**	mehm
better	**mieux**	mee-uh
here / everywhere	**ici / partout**	ee-see / par-too

Assorted beginnings and endings:

I like...	**J'aime...**	zhehm
I don't like...	**Je n'aime pas...**	zhuh nehm pah
Do you like...?	**Aimez-vous...?**	eh-may-voo
In the past...	**Au passé...**	oh pah-say
I am / Are you...?	**Je suis / Êtes-vous...?**	zhuh swee / eht-voo
...optimistic / pessimistic	**...optimiste / pessimiste**	zohp-tee-meest / peh-see-meest
I believe...	**Je crois...**	zhuh krwah
I don't believe...	**Je ne crois pas...**	zhuh nuh krwah pah
Do you believe...?	**Croyez-vous...?**	krwah-yay-voo
...in God	**...en Dieu**	ahn dee-uh
...in life after death	**...en la vie après la mort**	ahn lah vee ah-preh lah mor
...in extraterrestrial life	**...dans la vie extraterrestre**	dahn lah vee ehk-strah-tuh-rehs-truh
...in Santa Claus	**...au Père Noël**	oh pehr noh-ehl
Yes. / No.	**Oui. / Non.**	wee / nohn
Maybe.	**Peut-être.**	puh-teh-truh
I don't know.	**Je ne sais pas.**	zhuh nuh say pah
What's most important in life?	**Quel est le plus important dans la vie?**	kehl ay luh plewz an-por-tahn dahn lah vee

The problem is...	**Le problème, c'est que...**	luh proh-blehm say kuh
The answer is...	**La solution, c'est...**	luh soh-lew-see-oh<u>n</u> say
We have solved the world's problems.	**Nous avons résolu les problèmes du monde.**	nooz ah-voh<u>n</u> ray-zoh-lew lay proh-blehm dew moh<u>n</u>d

The French political scene:
These are the top six political parties in France, listed the same way you read, from left to right.

Parti Communiste: Beloved by labor unions, the communist party gets about a tenth of the vote.
Parti Écologiste: Also known as *Les Vert* ("the greens"), this is France's environmental party.
Parti Socialiste: The socialist party, led by Leonil Jospin, is France's mainstream left-leaning party.
Union Democrat Français (UDF): This business-oriented conservative party powered France in the 1970's. Remember Valery Giscard d'Estaing?
Républicains pour la Rassemblement (RPR): Founded by Charles de Gaulle and led by Jacques Chirac and Edouard Balladur, this traditionally conservative party vies with the Parti Socialiste for control.
Front National: Headed by Jean-Marie le Pen, this racist extreme right party advocates deportation of North African residents. Drawing about 10-15% of the vote, this party is fueled mainly by France's rural southern regions.

CHATTING

A French romance

Words of love:

I / me / you	**je / moi / tu**	zhuh / mwah / tew
flirt	**flirter**	fleer-tay
kiss	**baiser**	bay-zay
hug	**étreinte**	ay-tra<u>n</u>t
love	**amour**	ah-moor
make love	**faire l'amour**	fair lah-moor
condom	**préservatif**	pray-zehr-vah-teef
contraceptive	**contraceptif**	koh<u>n</u>-trah-sehp-teef
safe sex	**safe sex**	"safe sex"
sexy	**sexy**	"sexy"
cozy	**douillet**	doo-yay
romantic	**romantique**	roh-mah<u>n</u>-teek
my angel	**mon ange**	moh<u>n</u> ah<u>n</u>zh
my doe	**ma biche**	mah beesh
my pussy cat	**mon chat**	moh<u>n</u> shah
my little cabbage	**mon petit chou**	moh<u>n</u> puh-tee shoo

Ah, l'amour:

What's the matter?	**Qu'est-ce qu'il y a?**	kehs keel yah
Nothing.	**Rien.**	ree-a<u>n</u>
I am / Are you...?	**Je suis / Êtes-vous...?**	zhuh swee / eht voo
...gay	**...pédé**	pay-day
...straight	**...hétéro**	ay-tay-roh
...undecided	**...indécis**	a<u>n</u>-day-see

...prudish (m / f)	...pudibond / pudibonde	pew-dee-bohn / pew-dee-bohnd
...horny	...excité	ehk-see-tay
We are on our honeymoon.	C'est notre lune de miel.	say noh-truh lewn duh mee-ehl
I have a boyfriend.	J'ai un petit ami.	zhay uhn puh-tee tah-mee
I have a girlfriend.	J'ai une petite amie.	zhay ewn puh-tee tah-mee
I'm married.	Je suis marié.	zhuh swee mah-ree-ay
I'm not married.	Je ne suis pas marié.	zhuh nuh swee pah mah-ree-ay
I am rich and single.	Je suis riche et célibataire.	zhuh swee reesh ay say-lee-bah-tair
I'm lonely.	Je m'ennuie.	zhuh mahn-nwee
I have no diseases.	Je n'ai pas de maladies.	zhuh nay pah duh mah-lah-dee
I have many diseases.	J'ai plusieurs maladies.	zhay plewz-yur mah-lah-dee
Can I see you again?	On peut se revoir?	ohn puh suh ruh-vwahr
You are my most beautiful souvenir.	Vous êtes mon plus beau souvenir.	vooz eht mohn plew boh soo-vuh-neer
Is this an aphrodisiac?	C'est un aphrodisiaque?	sayt uhn ah-froh-dee-zee-yahk
This is my first time.	C'est la première fois.	say lah pruhm-yehr fwah
This is not my first time.	Ce n'est pas la première fois.	seh nay pah lah pruhm-yehr fwah
Do you do this often?	Vous ça faites souvent?	voo suh fayt soo-vahn
How's my breath?	Comment trouvez-vous mon haleine?	koh-mahn troo-vay-voo mohn ah-lehn
Let's just be friends.	Soyons amis.	swah-yohnz ah-mee

CHATTING

I'll pay for my share.	**Je pale mon écot.**	zhuh pay moh<u>n</u> ay-koh
Would you like a massage...?	**Voulez-vous un massage...?**	voo-lay-voo uh<u>n</u> mah-sahzh
...for your back	**...pour le dos**	poor luh doh
...for your feet	**...des pieds**	day pee-yay
Why not?	**Pourquoi pas?**	poor-kwah pah
Try it.	**Essayez-le.**	eh-say-yay-luh
That tickles.	**Ça chatouille.**	sah shah-too-ee
Oh my God.	**Mon Dieu.**	moh<u>n</u> dee-uh
I love you.	**Je t'aime.**	zhuh tehm
Darling, will you marry me?	**Chéri, veux-tu m'épouser?**	shay-ree vuh-tew may-poo-zay

English - French Dictionary

A

above au dessus
accident accident
accountant comptable
adaptor adapteur
address adresse
adult adulte
afraid peur
after après
afternoon après-midi
aftershave après rasage
afterwards après
again encore
age âge
aggressive aggressif
agree d'accord
AIDS SIDA
air l'air
air-conditioned climatisé
airline ligne aérienne
air mail par avion
airport aéroport
alarm clock réveille-matin
alcohol alcool
allergic allergique
allergies allergies
alone seule
already déjà
always toujours
ancestor ancêtre
ancient ancien
and et
angry fâché

ankle cheville
animal animal
another encore
answer réponse
antibiotic antibiotique
antiques antiquités
apartment appartement
apology excuses
appetizers hors-d'oeuvre
apple pomme
appointment rendez-vous
approximately presque
arm bras
arrivals arrivées
arrive arriver
art l'art
artificial artificial
artist artiste
ashtray cendrier
ask demander
aspirin aspirine
at à
attractive attirant
aunt tante
Austria Autriche
autumn automne

B

baby bébé
babysitter babysitter
backpack sac à dos
bad mauvais

bag sac
baggage bagages
bakery boulangerie
balcony balcon
ball balle
banana banane
band-aid bandage adhésif
bank banque
barber coiffeur
basement sous-sol
basket pannier
bath bain
bathroom salle de bain
bathtub baignoire
battery batterie
beach plage
beard barbe
beautiful belle
because parce que
bed lit
bedroom chambre
bedsheet draps
beef boeuf
beer bière
before avant
begin commencer
behind derrière
below sous
belt ceinture
best le meilleur
better meilleur
bib bavoir
bicycle vélo
big grand
bill (payment) addition
bird oiseau

birthday anniversaire
black noir
blanket couverture
blond blonde
blood sang
blue bleu
boat bateau
body corps
boiled bouilli
bomb bombe
book livre
book shop librairie
boots bottes
border frontière
borrow emprunter
boss chef
bottle bouteille
bottom fond
bowl bol
box boîte
boy garçon
bra soutien-gorge
bracelet bracelet
bread pain
breakfast petit déjeuner
bridge pont
briefs slip
Britain Grande-Bretagne
broken en panne
brother frère
brown brun
bucket seau
building bâtiment
bulb ampoule
burn (n) brûlure
bus bus

business affaires
business card carte de visite
but mais
button bouton
buy acheter
by (via) en

C

calendar calendrier
calorie calorie
camera appareil-photo
camping camping
can (n) boîte de conserve
can (v) pouvoir
can opener ouvre-boîte
Canada Canada
canal canal
candle chandelle
candy bonbon
canoe canoë
cap casquette
captain capitaine
car voiture
carafe carafe
card carte
cards (deck) jeu de cartes
careful prudent
carpet moquette
carry porter
cashier caisse
cassette cassette
castle château
cat chat
catch (v) attraper
cathedral cathédrale

cave grotte
cellar cave
center centre
century siècle
chair chaise
change (n) change
change (v) changer
charming charmant
cheap bon marché
check chèque
Cheers! Santé!
cheese fromage
chicken poulet
children enfants
Chinese (adj) chinois
chocolate chocolat
Christmas Noël
church église
cigarette cigarette
cinema cinéma
city ville
class classe
clean (adj) propre
clear clair
cliff falaise
closed fermé
cloth tissu
clothes vêtements
clothes pins pince à linge
clothesline corde à linge
cloudy nuageux
coast côte
coat hanger cintre
coffee café
coins pièces
cold (adj) froid

DICTIONARY

colors couleurs
comb (n) peigne
come venir
comfortable confortable
compact disc disque compact
complain se plaindre
complicated compliqué
computer ordinateur
concert concert
condom préservatif
conductor conducteur
confirm confirmer
congratulations félicitations
connection (train)
    correspondance
constipation constipation
cook (v) cuisinier
cool frais
cork bouchon
corkscrew tire-bouchon
corner coin
corridor couloir
cost (v) coûter
cot lit de camp
cotton coton
cough (v) tousser
cough drop pastille
country pays
countryside compagne
cousin cousin
cow vâche
cozy confortable
crafts arts
cream crème
credit card carte de crédit
crowd (n) foule

cry (v) pleurer
cup tasse

D

dad papa
dance (v) danser
danger danger
dangerous dangereux
dark sombre
daughter fille
day jour
dead mort
delay retardement
delicious délicieux
dental floss fil dentaire
dentist dentiste
deodorant désodorisant
depart partir
departures départs
deposit caution
dessert dessert
detour déviation
diabetic diabétique
diamond diamant
diaper couche
diarrhea diarrhée
dictionary dictionnaire
die mourir
difficult difficile
dinner dîner
direct direct
direction direction
dirty sale
discount réduction
disease maladie

disturb déranger
divorced divorcé
doctor docteur
dog chien
doll poupée
donkey âne
door porte
dormitory dortoire
double double
down en bas
dream (n) rêve
dream (v) rêver
dress (n) robe
drink (n) boisson
drive (v) conduire
driver chauffeur
drunk ivre
dry sec

E

each chaque
ear oreille
early tôt
earplugs boules quiès
earrings boucle d'oreille
earth terre
east est
Easter Pâques
easy facile
eat manger
elbow coude
elevator ascenseur
embarrassing gênant
embassy ambassade
empty vide

engineer ingénieur
English anglais
enjoy apprécier
enough assez
entrance entrée
entry entrée
envelope enveloppe
eraser gomme
especially spécialement
Europe Europe
evening soir
every chaque
everything tout
exactly exactement
example exemple
excellent excellent
except sauf
exchange (n) change
excuse me pardon
exhausted épuisé
exit sortie
expensive cher
explain expliquer
eye oeil

F

face visage
factory usine
fall (v) tomber
false faux
family famille
famous fameux
fantastic fantastique
far loin
farm ferme

farmer fermier
fashion mode
fat (adj) gros
father père
father-in-law beau-père
faucet robinet
fax fax
female femelle
ferry bac
fever fièvre
few peu
field champ
fight (v) combattre
fight (n) lutte
fine (good) bon
finger doigt
finish (v) finir
fireworks feux d'artifices
first premier
first aid premiers secours
first class première classe
fish (v) pêcher
fish poisson
fix (v) réparer
fizzy pétillant
flag drapeau
flashlight lampe de poche
flavor (n) parfum
flea puce
flight vol
flower fleur
flu grippe
fly voler
fog brouillard
food nourriture
foot pied

football football
for pour
forbidden interdit
foreign étranger
forget oublier
fork fourchette
fountain fontaine
free (no cost) gratuit
French francais
fresh fraîche
Friday vendredi
friend ami
friendship amitié
frisbee frisbee
from de
fruit fruit
fun amusement
funeral enterrement
funny drôle
furniture meubles
future avenir

G

gallery gallerie
game jeu
garage garage
garden jardin
gardening jardinage
gas essence
gas station station de service
gay homosexuel
gentleman monsieur
genuine authentique
Germany Allemagne
gift cadeau

girl fille
give donner
glass verre
glasses (eye) lunettes
gloves gants
go aller
go through passer
God Dieu
gold or
golf golf
good bien
good day bonjour
goodbye au revoir
grammar grammaire
granddaughter petite-fille
grandfather grand-père
grandmother grand-mère
grandson petit-fils
gray gris
greasy graisseux
great super
Greece Grèce
green vert
grocery store épicerie
guarantee garantie
guest invité
guide guide
guidebook guide
guitar guitare
gum chewing-gum
gun fusil

H

hair cheveux
hairbrush brosse

haircut coupe de cheveux
hand main
handicapped handicapé
handicrafts produits artisanaux
handle (n) poignée
handsome beau
happy heureux
harbor port
hard dûr
hat chapeau
hate (v) détester
have avoir
he il
head tête
headache mal de tête
healthy bonne santé
hear entendre
heart coeur
heat (n) chauffage
heat (v) chauffer
heaven paradis
heavy lourd
hello bonjour
help (v) aider
help (n) secours
hemorrhoids hémorroïdes
her elle
here ici
hi salut
high haut
highchair chaise haute
highway grande route
hill colline
history histoire
hitchhike autostop
hobby hobby

DICTIONARY

hole trou
holiday jour férié
homemade fait à la maison
homesick nostalgique
honest honnête
honeymoon lune de miel
horrible horrible
horse cheval
horse riding équitation
hospital hôpital
hot chaud
hotel hôtel
hour heure
house maison
how comment
how many combien
how much ($) combien
hungry faim
hurry (v) se dépêcher
husband mari
hydrofoil hydroptère

independent indépendant
indigestion indigestion
industry industrie
information information
injured blessé
innocent innocent
insect insecte
insect repellant bombe contre
  les insectes
inside dedans
instant instant
instead au lieu
insurance assurance
intelligent intelligent
interesting intéressant
invitation invitation
iodine teinture d'iode
is est
island île
Italy Italie
itch (n) démangeaison

I

I je
ice glaçons
ice cream glace
if si
ill malade
immediately immédiatement
important important
imported importé
impossible impossible
in en, dans
included inclus
incredible incroyable

J

jacket veste
jaw machoire
jeans jeans
jewelry bijoux
job boulot
jogging jogging
joke (n) blague
journey voyage
juice jus
jump (v) sauter

K

keep garder
kettle bouilloire
key clé
kill tuer
kind aimable
king roi
kiss (n) baiser
kitchen cuisine
knee genou
knife couteau
know savoir

L

ladder échelle
ladies mesdames
lake lac
lamb agneau
language langue
large grand
last dernier
late tard
later plus tard
laugh (v) rire
laundromat laverie
lawyer avocat
lazy paresseux
leather cuir
leave partir
left gauche
leg jambe
lend prêter
letter lettre

library bibliothèque
life vie
light (n) lumière
light bulb ampoule
lighter (n) briquet
like aimer bien
lip lèvre
list liste
listen écouter
liter litre
little (adj) petit
local régional
lock (v) fermer à clé
lock (n) serrure
lockers consigne
look regarder
lost perdu
loud bruyant
love (v) aimer
lover amant
low bas
lozenges pastilles
luck chance
luggage bagage
lukewarm tiède
lungs poumons

M

macho macho
mad fâché
magazine magazine
mail (n) courrier
main principal
make (v) faire
male mâle

man homme
manager directeur
many beaucoup
map carte
market marché
married marié
matches allumettes
maximum maximum
maybe peut-être
meat viande
medicine médicaments
medium moyen
men hommes
menu carte
message message
metal métal
midnight minuit
mild doux
mineral water eau minérale
minimum minimum
minutes minutes
mirror miroir
Miss Mademoiselle
mistake erreur
misunderstanding malentendu
mix (n) mélange
modern moderne
moment moment
Monday lundi
money argent
month mois
monument monument
moon lune
more encore
morning matin
mosquito moustique
mother mère

mother-in-law belle mère
mountain montagne
moustache moustache
mouth bouche
movie film
Mr. Monsieur
Mrs. Madame
much beaucoup
muscle muscle
museum musée
music musique
my mon, ma

N

nail clipper pince à ongles
naked nu
name nom
napkin serviette
narrow étroit
nationality nationalité
natural naturel
nature nature
nausea nausée
near près
necessary nécessaire
necklace collier
need avoir besoin de
needle aiguille
nephew neveu
nervous nerveux
never jamais
new nouveau
newspaper journal
next prochain
nice plaisant

nickname sobriquet
niece nièce
night nuit
no non
no vacancy complet
noisy bruillant
non-smoking non fumeur
noon midi
normal normale
north nord
nose nez
not pas
notebook calepin
nothing rien
now maintenant

O

occupation emploi
occupied occupé
ocean océan
of de
office bureau
OK d'accord
old vieux
on sur
once une fois
one way (street) sens unique
one way (ticket) aller simple
only seulement
open (adj) ouvert
open (v) ouvrir
opera opéra
operator standardiste
optician opticien
or ou

orange (color) orange
orange (fruit) orange
original original
other autre
outdoors en plein air
oven four
over (finished) fini
own posséder
owner propriétaire

P

pacifier tétine
package colis
page page
pail seau
pain douleur
painting tableau
palace palais
panties slip
pants pantalon
paper papier
paper clip trombone
parents parents
park (v) garer
park (garden) parc
party soirée
passenger passager
passport passeport
pay payer
peace paix
pedestrian piéton
pen stylo
pencil crayon
people gens
percent pourcentage

perfect parfait
perfume parfum
period (time) période
period (woman's) règles
person personne
pharmacy pharmacie
photo photo
pick-pocket pickpocket
picnic pique-nique
piece morceau
pig cochon
pill pilule
pillow oreiller
pin épingle
pink rose
pity, it's a quel dommage
pizza pizza
plain simple
plane avion
plant plante
plastic plastique
plastic bag sac en plastique
plate assiette
platform (train) quai
play (v) jouer
play théâtre
please s'il vous plaît
pliers pinces
pocket poche
point (v) indiquer
police police
poor pauvre
pork porc
possible possible
postcard carte postale
poster affiche
practical pratique

pregnant enceinte
prescription ordonnance
present (gift) cadeau
pretty jolie
price prix
priest prêtre
private privé
problem problème
profession profession
prohibited interdit
pronunciation prononciation
public publique
pull tirer
purple violet
purse sac
push pousser

Q

quality qualité
quarter (¼) quart
queen reine
question (n) question
quiet silence

R

R.V. camping-car
rabbit lapin
radio radio
raft radeau
railway chemin de fer
rain (n) pluie
rainbow arc-en-ciel
raincoat imperméable
rape (n) viol

raw cru
razor rasoir
ready prêt
receipt reçu
receive recevoir
receptionist réceptioniste
recipe recette
recommend suggérer
red rouge
refill (v) remplir
refund (n) remboursement
relax (v) se reposer
religion religion
remember se souvenir
rent (v) louer
repair (v) réparer
repeat (v) répéter
reservation réservation
reserve reserver
rich riche
right droite
ring (n) bague
ripe mûr
river rivière
rock (n) rocher
roller skates patins à roulettes
romantic romantique
roof toit
room chambre
rope corde
rotten pourri
round trip aller-retour
rowboat canot
rucksack sac à dos
rug tapis
ruins ruines
run (v) courir

S

sad triste
safe en sécurité
safety pin épingle à nourrice
sailing voile
sale solde
same même
sandals sandales
sandwich sandwich
sanitary napkins serviettes
  hygiéniques
Saturday samedi
scandalous scandaleux
school école
science science
scientist homme / femme de
  sciences
scissors ciseaux
scotch tape du scotch
screwdriver tournevis
sculptor sculpteur
sculpture sculpture
sea mer
seafood fruits de mer
seat place
second deuxième
second class deuxième classe
secret secret
see voir
self-service libre service
sell vendre
send envoyer
separate (adj) séparé
serious sérieux
service service

sex sexe
sexy sexy
shampoo shampooing
shaving cream crème à raser
she elle
sheet drap
shell coquille
ship (n) navire
shirt chemise
shoes chaussures
shopping shopping
short court
shorts short
shoulder épaule
show (v) montrer
show (n) spectacle
shower douche
shy timide
sick malade
sign panneau
signature signature
silence silence
silk soie
silver argent
similar semblable
simple simple
sing chanter
singer chanteur
single célibataire
sink lavabo
sir monsieur
sister soeur
size taille
skating patinage
ski (v) faire du ski
skin peau
skinny maigre

skirt jupe
sky ciel
sleep (v) dormir
sleepy avoir sommeil
slice tranche
slide (photo) diapositive
slippery glissant
slow lent
small petit
smell (n) odeur
smile (v) sourire
smoking fumeur
snack snack
sneeze (v) éternuer
snore ronfler
soap savon
soccer football
socks chaussettes
something quelque chose
son fils
song chanson
soon bientôt
sorry désolé
sour aigre
south sud
speak parler
specialty spécialité
speed vitesse
spend dépenser
spicy piquant
spider araignée
spoon cuillère
sport sport
spring printemps
square (town) place
stairs escalier
stamp timbre

stapler agraffeuse
star (in sky) étoile
state état
station station
stomach estomac
stop (v) arrêter
stop (n) stop, arrêt
storm tempête
story (floor) étage
straight droit
strange bizarre
stream (n) ruisseau
street rue
string ficelle
strong fort
stuck coincé
student étudiant
stupid stupide
sturdy robuste
style mode
suddenly soudain
suitcase valise
summer été
sun soleil
sunbathe se faire bronzer
sunburn coup de soleil
Sunday dimanche
sunglasses lunettes de soleil
sunny ensoleillé
sunset coucher de soleil
sunscreen huile solaire
sunshine soleil
sunstroke insolation
suntan (n) bronzage
suntan lotion lotion solaire
supermarket supermarché
supplement supplément

surprise (n) surprise
swallow (v) avaler
sweat (v) transpirer
sweater pull
sweet doux
swim nager
swim trunks maillot de bain
swimming pool piscine
swimsuit costume de bain
Switzerland Suisse
synthetic synthétique

T

table table
tail queue
take prendre
take out (food) emporter
talcum powder talc
talk parler
tall grand
tampons tampons
tape (cassette) cassette
taste (n) goût
taste (v) goûter
tax taxe
teacher professeur
team équipe
teenager adolescent
telephone téléphone
television télévision
temperature température
tender tendre
tennis tennis
tennis shoes chaussures de tennis

DICTIONARY

tent tente
tent pegs piquets de tente
terrible terrible
thanks merci
theater théâtre
thermometer thermomètre
thick épais
thief voleur
thigh cuisse
thin mince
thing chose
think penser
thirsty soif
thongs pinces
thread fil
throat gorge
through à travers
throw jeter
Thursday jeudi
ticket billet
tight serré
timetable horaire
tired fatigué
tissues mouchoirs en papier
to à
today aujourd'hui
toe orteil
together ensemble
toilet toilette
toilet paper papier hygiénique
tomorrow demain
tonight ce soir
too (much) trop
tooth dent
toothbrush brosse à dents
toothpaste dentifrice
toothpick cure-dent

total total
touch (v) toucher
tough dur
tour tour
tourist touriste
towel serviette de bain
tower tour
town village
toy jouet
track (train) voie
traditional traditionnel
traffic circulation
train train
translate traduire
travel voyager
travel agency agence de voyage
travelers check chèque de voyage
tree arbre
trip voyage
trouble trouble
T-shirt T-shirt
Tuesday mardi
tunnel tunnel
tweezers pince à épiler
twins jumeaux

U

ugly laid
umbrella parapluie
uncle oncle
under sous
underpants slip
understand comprendre

underwear sous vêtements
unemployed au chômage
unfortunately malheureusement
United States Etats-Unis
university univerisité
up en haut
upstairs en haut
urgent urgent
us nous
use utiliser

V

vacancy (hotel) chambre libre
vacant libre
valley vallée
vegetarian (n) végétarien
very très
vest gilet
video vidéo
video recorder magnétoscope
view vue
village village
vineyard vignoble
virus virus
visit (n) visite
visit (v) visiter
vitamins vitamines
voice voix
vomit (v) vomir

W

waist taille
wait attendre
waiter garçon

waitress serveuse
wake up se réveiller
walk (v) marcher
wallet portefeuille
want vouloir
warm (adj) chaud
wash laver
watch (n) montre
watch (v) regarder
water eau
water, tap eau du robinet
waterfall cascade
we nous
weather temps
weather forecast météo
wedding mariage
Wednesday mercredi
week semaine
weight poids
welcome bienvenue
west ouest
wet mouillé
what que
wheel roue
when quand
where où
whipped cream crème chantilly
white blanc
who qui
why pourquoi
widow veuve
widower veuf
wife femme
wild sauvage
wind vent
window fenêtre

wine   vin
wing   aile
winter   hiver
wish (v)   souhaiter
with   avec
without   sans
women   dames
wood   bois
wool   laine
word   mot
work (n)   travail
work (v)   travailler
world   monde
worse   pire
worst   le pire
wrap   emballer
wrist   poignet
write   écrire

Y

year   année
yellow   jaune
yes   oui
yesterday   hier
you (formal)   vous
you (informal)   tu
young   jeune
youth hostel   auberge de jeunesse

Z

zero   zero
zip-lock bag   sac en plastique à fermeture
zipper   fermeture éclair
zoo   zoo

French-English Dictionary

A

à   at
à   to
à travers   through
accident   accident
acheter   buy
adapteur   adaptor
addition   bill (payment)
adolescent   teenager
adresse   address
adulte   adult
aéroport   airport
affaires   business
affiche   poster
âge   age
agence de voyage   travel agency
aggressif   aggressive
agneau   lamb
agraffeuse   stapler
aider   help (v)
aigre   sour
aiguille   needle
aile   wing
aimable   kind
aimer   love (v)
aimer bien   like
alcool   alcohol
Allemagne   Germany
aller   go
aller-retour   round trip
aller simple   one way (ticket)
allergies   allergies

allergique   allergic
allumettes   matches
amant   lover
ambassade   embassy
ami   friend
amitié   friendship
ampoule   bulb
ampoule   light bulb
amusement   fun
ancêtre   ancestor
ancien   ancient
âne   donkey
anglais   English
animal   animal
année   year
anniversaire   birthday
antibiotique   antibiotic
antiquités   antiques
appareil-photo   camera
appartement   apartment
apprécier   enjoy
après   after
après   afterwards
après-midi   afternoon
après rasage   aftershave
araignée   spider
arbre   tree
arc-en-ciel   rainbow
argent   money
argent   silver
arrêter   stop (v)
arrivées   arrivals
arriver   arrive
artificial   artificial

DICTIONARY

artiste artist
arts crafts
ascenseur elevator
aspirine aspirin
assez enough
assiette plate
assurance insurance
attendre wait
attirant attractive
attraper catch (v)
au chômage unemployed
au dessus above
au lieu instead
au revoir goodbye
auberge de jeunesse youth hostel
aujourd'hui today
authentique genuine
automne autumn
autostop hitchhike
autre other
Autriche Austria
avaler swallow (v)
avant before
avec with
avenir future
avion plane
avocat lawyer
avoir have
avoir besoin de need
avoir sommeil sleepy

B

babysitter babysitter
bac ferry

bagage luggage
bagages baggage
bague ring (n)
baignoire bathtub
bain bath
baiser kiss (n)
balcon balcony
balle ball
banane banana
bandage adhésif band-aid
banque bank
barbe beard
bas low
bateau boat
bâtiment building
batterie battery
bavoir bib
beau handsome
beau-père father-in-law
beaucoup many
beaucoup much
bébé baby
belle beautiful
belle mère mother-in-law
bibliothèque library
bien good
bientôt soon
bienvenue welcome
bière beer
bijoux jewelry
billet ticket
bizarre strange
blagu joke (n)
blanc white
blessé injured
bleu blue

blonde blond
boeuf beef
bois wood
boisson drink (n)
boîte box
boîte de conserve can (n)
bol bowl
bombe bomb
bombe contre les insectes insect repellant
bon fine (good)
bon marché cheap
bonbon candy
bonjour good day
bonjour hello
bonne santé healthy
bottes boots
bouche mouth
bouchon cork
boucle d'oreille earrings
bouilli boiled
bouilloire kettle
boulangerie bakery
boules quiès earplugs
boulot job
bouteille bottle
bouton button
bracelet bracelet
bras arm
briquet lighter (n)
bronzage suntan (n)
brosse hairbrush
brosse à dents toothbrush
brouillard fog
bruillant noisy
brûlure burn (n)
brun brown

bruyant loud
bureau office
bus bus

C

cadeau gift
cadeau present (gift)
café coffee
caisse cashier
calendrier calendar
calepin notebook
calorie calorie
camping camping
camping-car R.V.
Canada Canada
canal canal
canoë canoe
canot rowboat
capitaine captain
carafe carafe
carte card
carte map
carte menu
carte de crédit credit card
carte de visite business card
carte postale postcard
cascade waterfall
casquette cap
cassette cassette
cassette tape (cassette)
cathédrale cathedral
cave cellar
ce soir tonight
ceinture belt
célibataire single

cendrier ashtray
centre center
chaise chair
chaise haute highchair
chambre bedroom
chambre room
chambre libre vacancy (hotel)
champ field
chance luck
chandelle candle
change change (n)
change exchange (n)
changer change (v)
chanson song
chanter sing
chanteur singer
chapeau hat
chaque each
chaque every
charmant charming
chat cat
château castle
chaud hot
chaud warm (adj)
chauffage heat (n)
chauffer heat (v)
chauffeur driver
chaussettes socks
chaussures shoes
chaussures de tennis tennis shoes
chef boss
chemin de fer railway
chemise shirt
chèque check
chèque de voyage travelers check

cher expensive
cheval horse
cheveux hair
cheville ankle
chewing-gum gum
chien dog
chinois Chinese (adj)
chocolat chocolate
chose thing
ciel sky
cigarette cigarette
cinéma cinema
cintre coat hanger
circulation traffic
ciseaux scissors
clair clear
classe class
clé key
climatisé air-conditioned
cochon pig
coeur heart
coiffeur barber
coin corner
coincé stuck
colis package
collier necklace
colline hill
combattre fight (v)
combien how many
combien how much ($)
commencer begin
comment how
compagne countryside
complet no vacancy
compliqué complicated
comprendre understand
comptable accountant

concert concert
conducteur conductor
conduire drive (v)
confirmer confirm
confortable comfortable
confortable cozy
consigne lockers
constipation constipation
coquille shell
corde rope
corde à linge clothesline
corps body
correspondance connection (train)
costume de bain swim suit
côte coast
coton cotton
couche diaper
coucher de soleil sunset
coude elbow
couleurs colors
couloir corridor
coup de soleil sunburn
coupe de cheveux haircut
courir run (v)
courrier mail (n)
court short
cousin cousin
couteau knife
coûter cost (v)
couverture blanket
crayon pencil
crème cream
crème à raser shaving cream
crème chantilly whipped cream
cru raw

cuillère spoon
cuir leather
cuisine kitchen
cuisinier cook (v)
cuisse thigh
cure-dent toothpick

D

d'accord agree
d'accord OK
dames women
danger danger
dangereux dangerous
danser dance (v)
de from
de of
dedans inside
déjà already
délicieux delicious
demain tomorrow
demander ask
démangeaison itch (n)
dent tooth
dentifrice toothpaste
dentiste dentist
départs departures
dépenser spend
dépôt deposit
déranger disturb
dernier last
derrière behind
désodorisant deodorant
désolé sorry
dessert dessert
détester hate (v)

deuxième second
deuxième classe second class
déviation detour
diabétique diabetic
diamant diamond
diapositive slide (photo)
diarrhée diarrhea
dictionnaire dictionary
Dieu God
difficile difficult
dimanche Sunday
dîner dinner
direct direct
directeur manager
direction direction
disque compact compact disc
divorcé divorced
docteur doctor
doigt finger
donner give
dormir sleep (v)
dortoire dormitory
double double
douche shower
douleur pain
doux mild
doux sweet
drap sheet
drapeau flag
draps bedsheet
droit straight
droite right
drôle funny
du scotch scotch tape
dûr hard
dur tough

E

eau water
eau du robinet water, tap
eau minérale mineral water
échelle ladder
école school
écouter listen
écrire write
église church
elle her
elle she
emballer wrap
emploi occupation
emporter take out (food)
emprunter borrow
en by (via)
en bas down
en, dans in
en haut up
en haut upstairs
en panne broken
en plein air outdoors
en sécurité safe
enceinte pregnant
encore again
encore another
encore more
enfants children
ensemble together
ensoleillé sunny
entendre hear
enterrement funeral
entrée entrance
entrée entry
enveloppe envelope

envoyer   send
épais   thick
épaule   shoulder
épicerie   grocery store
épingle   pin
épingle à nourrice   safety pin
épuisé   exhausted
équipe   team
équitation   horse riding
erreur   mistake
escalier   stairs
essence   gas
est   east
est   is
estomac   stomach
et   and
étage   story (floor)
état   state
Etats-Unis   United States
été   summer
éternuer   sneeze (v)
étoile   star (in sky)
étranger   foreign
étroit   narrow
étudiant   student
Europe   Europe
exactement   exactly
excellent   excellent
excuses   apology
exemple   example
expliquer   explain

F

fâché   angry
fâché   mad

facile   easy
faim   hungry
faire   make (v)
faire du ski   ski (v)
fait à la maison   homemade
falaise   cliff
fameux   famous
famille   family
fantastique   fantastic
fatigué   tired
faux   false
fax   fax
félicitations   congratulations
femelle   female
femme   wife
fenêtre   window
fermé   closed
ferme   farm
fermer à clé   lock (v)
fermeture éclair   zipper
fermier   farmer
feux d'artifices   fireworks
ficelle   string
fièvre   fever
fil   thread
fil dentaire   dental floss
fille   daughter
fille   girl
film   movie
fils   son
fini   over (finished)
finir   finish (v)
fleur   flower
fond   bottom
fontaine   fountain
football   football
football   soccer

fort strong
foule crowd (n)
four oven
fourchette fork
fraîche fresh
frais cool
francais French
frère brother
frisbee frisbee
froid cold (adj)
fromage cheese
frontière border
fruit fruit
fruits de mer seafood
fumeur smoking
fusil gun

G

gallerie gallery
gants gloves
garage garage
garçon boy
garçon waiter
garder keep
garer park (v)
gauche left
gênant embarrassing
genou knee
gens people
gilet vest
glace ice cream
glaçons ice
glissant slippery
golf golf
gomme eraser

gorge throat
goût taste (n)
goûter taste (v)
graisseux greasy
grammaire grammar
grand big
grand large
grand tall
grand-mère grandmother
grand-père grandfather
Grande-Bretagne Britain
grande route highway
gratuit free (no cost)
Grèce Greece
grippe flu
gris gray
gros fat (adj)
grotte cave
guarantie guarantee
guide guide
guide guidebook
guitare guitar

H

handicapé handicapped
haut high
hémorroïdes hemorrhoids
heure hour
heureux happy
hier yesterday
histoire history
hiver winter
hobby hobby
homme man

homme / femme de sciences scientist
hommes men
homosexuel gay
honnête honest
hôpital hospital
horaire timetable
horrible horrible
hors-d'oeuvre appetizers
hôtel hotel
huile solaire sunscreen
hydroptère hydrofoil

I

ici here
il he
île island
immédiatement immediately
imperméable raincoat
important important
importé imported
impossible impossible
inclus included
incroyable incredible
indépendant independent
indigestion indigestion
indiquer point (v)
industrie industry
information information
ingénieur engineer
innocent innocent
insecte insect
insolation sunstroke
instant instant
intelligent intelligent

interdit forbidden
interdit prohibited
intéressant interesting
invitation invitation
invité guest
Italie Italy
ivre drunk

J

jamais never
jambe leg
jardin garden
jardinage gardening
jaune yellow
je I
jeans jeans
jeter throw
jeu game
jeu de cartes cards (deck)
jeudi Thursday
jeune young
jogging jogging
jolie pretty
jouer play (v)
jouet toy
jour day
jour férié holiday
journal newspaper
jumeaux twins
jupe skirt
jus juice

L

l'air air
l'art art
lac lake
laid ugly
laine wool
lampe de poche flashlight
langue language
lapin rabbit
lavabo sink
laver wash
laverie laundromat
le meilleur best
le pire worst
lent slow
lettre letter
lèvre lip
librairie book shop
libre vacant
libre service self-service
ligne aérienne airline
liste list
lit bed
lit de camp cot
litre liter
livre book
loin far
lotion solaire suntan lotion
louer rent (v)
lourd heavy
lumière light (n)
lundi Monday
lune moon
lune de miel honeymoon
lunettes glasses (eye)
lunettes de soleil sunglasses
lutte fight (n)

M

macho macho
machoire jaw
Madame Mrs.
Mademoiselle Miss
magazine magazine
magnétoscope video recorder
maigre skinny
maillot de bain swim trunks
main hand
maintenant now
mais but
maison house
mal de tête headache
malade ill
malade sick
maladie disease
mâle male
malentendu misunderstanding
malheureusement unfortunately
manger eat
marché market
marcher walk (v)
mardi Tuesday
mari husband
mariage wedding
marié married
matin morning
mauvais bad
maximum maximum
médicaments medicine

meilleur better
mélange mix (n)
même same
mer sea
merci thanks
mercredi Wednesday
mère mother
mesdames ladies
message message
métal metal
météo weather forecast
meubles furniture
midi noon
mince thin
minimum minimum
minuit midnight
minutes minutes
miroir mirror
mode fashion
mode style
moderne modern
mois month
moment moment
mon, ma my
monde world
monsieur gentleman
Monsieur Mr.
monsieur sir
montagne mountain
montre watch (n)
montrer show (v)
monument monument
moquette carpet
morceau piece
mort dead
mot word
mouchoirs en papier tissues

mouillé wet
mourir die
moustache moustache
moustique mosquito
moyen medium
mûr ripe
muscle muscle
musée museum
musique music

N

nager swim
nationalité nationality
nature nature
naturel natural
nausée nausea
navire ship (n)
nécessaire necessary
nerveux nervous
neveu nephew
nez nose
nièce niece
Noël Christmas
noir black
nom name
non no
non fumeur non-smoking
nord north
normale normal
nostalgique homesick
nourriture food
nous us
nous we
nouveau new
nu naked

nuageux cloudy
nuit night

O

occupé occupied
océan ocean
odeur smell (n)
oeil eye
oiseau bird
oncle uncle
opéra opera
opticien optician
or gold
orange orange (color)
orange orange (fruit)
ordinateur computer
ordonnance prescription
oreille ear
oreiller pillow
original original
orteil toe
ou or
où where
oublier forget
ouest west
oui yes
ouvert open (adj)
ouvre-boîte can opener
ouvrir open (v)

P

page page
pain bread
paix peace

palais palace
panneau sign
pannier basket
pantalon pants
papa dad
papier paper
papier hygiénique toilet paper
Pâques Easter
par avion air mail
paradis heaven
parapluie umbrella
parc park (garden)
parce que because
pardon excuse me
parents parents
paresseux lazy
parfait perfect
parfum flavor (n)
parfum perfume
parler speak
parler talk
partir depart
partir leave
pas not
passager passenger
passeport passport
passer go through
pastille cough drop
pastilles lozenges
patinage skating
patins à roulettes roller skates
pauvre poor
payer pay
pays country
peau skin
pêcher fish (v)

peigne comb (n)
penser think
perdu lost
père father
période period (time)
personne person
pétillant fizzy
petit little (adj)
petit small
petit déjeuner breakfast
petit-fils grandson
petite-fille granddaughter
peu few
peur afraid
peut-être maybe
pharmacie pharmacy
photo photo
pickpocket pick-pocket
pièces coins
pied foot
piéton pedestrian
pilule pill
pince à épiler tweezers
pince à linge clothes pins
pince à ongles nail clipper
pinces pliers
pinces thongs
piquant spicy
pique-nique picnic
piquets de tente tent pegs
pire worse
piscine swimming pool
pizza pizza
place seat
place square (town)
plage beach

plaisant nice
plante plant
plastique plastic
pleurer cry (v)
pluie rain (n)
plus tard later
poche pocket
poids weight
poignée handle (n)
poignet wrist
poisson fish
police police
pomme apple
pont bridge
porc pork
port harbor
porte door
portefeuille wallet
porter carry
posséder own
possible possible
poulet chicken
poumons lungs
poupée doll
pour for
pourcentage percent
pourquoi why
pourri rotten
pousser push
pouvoir can (v)
pratique practical
premier first
première classe first class
premiers secours first aid
prendre take
près near

préservatif condom
presque approximately
prêt ready
prêter lend
prêtre priest
principal main
printemps spring
privé private
prix price
problème problem
prochain next
produits artisanaux handicrafts
professeur teacher
profession profession
prononciation pronunciation
propre clean (adj)
propriétaire owner
prudent careful
publique public
puce flea
pull sweater

Q

quai platform (train)
qualité quality
quand when
quart quarter (¼)
que what
quel dommage pity, it's a
quelque chose something
question question (n)
queue tail
qui who

R

radeau raft
radio radio
rasoir razor
réceptioniste receptionist
recette recipe
recevoir receive
reçu receipt
réduction discount
regarder look
regarder watch (v)
régional local
règles period (woman's)
reine queen
religion religion
remboursement refund (n)
remplir refill (v)
rendez-vous appointment
réparer fix (v)
réparer repair (v)
répéter repeat (v)
réponse answer
réservation reservation
reserver reserve
retardement delay
rêve dream (n)
réveille-matin alarm clock
rêver dream (v)
riche rich
rien nothing
rire laugh (v)
rivière river
robe dress (n)
robinet faucet
robuste sturdy

rocher rock (n)
roi king
romantique romantic
ronfler snore
rose pink
roue wheel
rouge red
rue street
ruines ruins
ruisseau stream (n)

S

s'il vous plaît please
sac bag
sac purse
sac à dos backpack
sac à dos rucksack
sac en plastique plastic bag
sac en plastique à fermeture
  zip-lock bag
sale dirty
salle de bain bathroom
salut hi
samedi Saturday
sandales sandals
sandwich sandwich
sang blood
sans without
Santé! Cheers!
sauf except
sauter jump (v)
sauvage wild
savoir know
savon soap
scandaleux scandalous

science science
sculpteur sculptor
sculpture sculpture
se dépêcher hurry (v)
se faire bronzer sunbathe
se plaindre complain
se reposer relax (v)
se réveiller wake up
se souvenir remember
seau bucket
seau pail
sec dry
secours help (n)
secret secret
semaine week
semblable similar
sens unique one way (street)
séparé separate (adj)
sérieux serious
serré tight
serrure lock (n)
serveuse waitress
service service
serviette napkin
serviette de bain towel
serviettes hygiéniques
  sanitary napkins
seule alone
seulement only
sexe sex
sexy sexy
shampooing shampoo
shopping shopping
short shorts
si if
SIDA AIDS

siècle century
signature signature
silence quiet
silence silence
simple plain
simple simple
slip briefs
slip panties
slip underpants
snack snack
sobriquet nickname
soeur sister
soie silk
soif thirsty
soir evening
soirée party
solde sale
soleil sun
soleil sunshine
sombre dark
sortie exit
soudain suddenly
souhaiter wish (v)
sourire smile (v)
sous below
sous under
sous-sol basement
sous vêtements underwear
soutien-gorge bra
spécialement especially
spécialité specialty
spectacle show (n)
sport sport
standardiste operator
station station
station de service gas station
stop, arrêt stop (n)

stupide stupid
stylo pen
sud south
suggérer recommend
Suisse Switzerland
super great
supermarché supermarket
supplément supplement
sur on
surprise surprise (n)
synthétique synthetic

T

T-shirt T-shirt
table table
tableau painting
taille size
taille waist
talc talcum powder
tampons tampons
tante aunt
tapis rug
tard late
tasse cup
taxe tax
teinture d'iode iodine
téléphone telephone
télévision television
température temperature
tempête storm
temps weather
tendre tender
tennis tennis
tente tent
terre earth

terrible terrible
tête head
tétine pacifier
théâtre play
théâtre theater
thermomètre thermometer
tiède lukewarm
timbre stamp
timide shy
tire-bouchon corkscrew
tirer pull
tissu cloth
toilette toilet
toit roof
tomber fall (v)
tôt early
total total
toucher touch (v)
toujours always
tour tour
tour tower
touriste tourist
tournevis screwdriver
tousser cough (v)
tout everything
traditionnel traditional
traduire translate
train train
tranche slice
transpirer sweat (v)
travail work (n)
travailler work (v)
très very
triste sad
trombone paper clip
trop too (much)

trou hole
trouble trouble
tu you (informal)
tuer kill
tunnel tunnel

U

une fois once
univerisité university
urgent urgent
usine factory
utiliser use

V

vâche cow
valise suitcase
vallée valley
végétarien vegetarian (n)
vélo bicycle
vendre sell
vendredi Friday
venir come
vent wind
verre glass
vert green
veste jacket
vêtements clothes
veuf widower
veuve widow
viande meat
vide empty
vidéo video
vie life

vieux old
vignoble vineyard
village town
village village
ville city
vin wine
viol rape (n)
violet purple
virus virus
visage face
visite visit (n)
visiter visit (v)
vitamines vitamins
vitesse speed
voie track (train)
voile sailing
voir see
voiture car
voix voice
vol flight
voler fly
voleur thief
vomir vomit (v)
vouloir want
vous you (formal)
voyage journey
voyage trip
voyager travel
vue view

Z

zero zero
zoo zoo

Hurdling the Language Barrier

Don't be afraid to communicate

Even the best phrase book won't satisfy your needs in every situation. To really hurdle the language barrier, you need to leap beyond the printed page, and dive into contact with the locals. Never allow your lack of foreign language skills to isolate you from the people and cultures you traveled halfway around the world to experience. Remember that in every country you visit, you're surrounded by expert, native-speaking tutors. Spend bus and train rides letting them teach you.

Start conversations by asking politely in the local language, "Do you speak English?" When you speak English with someone from another country, talk slowly, clearly, and with carefully chosen words. Use what the Voice of America calls "simple English." You're talking to people who are wishing it was written down, hoping to see each letter as it tumbles out of your mouth. Pronounce each letter, avoiding all contractions and slang. For bad examples, listen to other tourists.

Keep things caveman-simple. Make single nouns work as entire sentences ("Photo?"). Use internationally-understood words ("auto kaput" works in Bordeaux). Butcher the language if you must. The important thing is to make the effort. To get air mail stamps, you can flap your wings and say "tweet, tweet." If you want milk, moo and pull two imaginary udders. Risk looking like a fool.

If you're short on words, make your picnic a potluck. Pull out a map and point out your journey. Draw what you mean. Bring photos from home and introduce your family.

APPENDIX

Play cards or toss a Frisbee. Fold an origami bird for kids or dazzle 'em with sleight-of-hand magic.

Go ahead and make educated guesses. Many situations are easy-to-fake multiple choice questions. Practice. Read timetables, concert posters and newspaper headlines. Listen to each language on a multilingual tour. Be melodramatic. Exaggerate the local accent. Self-consciousness is the deadliest communication-killer.

Choose multilingual people to communicate with, like students, business people, urbanites, young well-dressed people, or anyone in the tourist trade. Use a small note pad to keep track of handy phrases you pick up—and to help you communicate more clearly with the locals by scribbling down numbers, maps, and so on. Some travelers carry important messages written on a small card: vegetarian, boiled water, your finest ice cream.

Numbers and Stumblers:

■ Europeans write a few numbers differently than we do. The one has an upswing (1), the four looks like a lightning bolt (4), and the seven has a cross (7).

■ Europeans write the date in this order: day/month/year. Christmas is 25-12-01, not 12-25-01.

■ Commas are decimal points and decimals are commas. A dollar and a half is 1,50 and 5.280 feet are in a mile.

■ The European "first floor" isn't the ground floor, but the first floor up.

■ When counting with your fingers, start with your thumb. If you hold up only your first finger, you'll probably get two of something.

International words

As our world shrinks, more and more words hop across their linguistic boundaries and become international. Savvy travelers develop a knack for choosing words most likely to be universally understood ("auto" instead of "car," "kaput" rather than "broken," "photo," not "picture"). Internationalize your pronunciation. "University," if you play around with its sound (oo-nee-vehr-see-tay), will be understood anywhere. Practice speaking English with a heavy French accent. Wave your arms a lot. Be creative.

Here are a few internationally understood words. Remember, cut out the Yankee accent and give each word a pan-European sound.

Stop	Kaput	Vino	Restaurant
Ciao	Bank	Hotel	Bye-bye
Rock 'n' roll	Post	Camping	OK
Auto	Picnic	Amigo	Autobus (boos)
Nuclear	Macho	Tourist	English
Yankee	Americano	Mama mia	Michelangelo
Beer	Oo la la	Coffee	Casanova (romantic)
Chocolate	Moment	Sexy	Disneyland
Tea	Coca-Cola	No problem	Passport
Telephone	Photo	Photocopy	Police
Europa	Self-service	Toilet	Information
Super	Taxi	Central	Rambo
Pardon	University	Fascist	U.S. profanity

French tongue twisters

Tongue twisters are a great way to practice a language—and break the ice with local Europeans. Here are a few French tongue twisters that are sure to challenge you, and amuse your hosts.

Bonjour madame la saucissonière! Combien sont ces six saucissons-ci? Ces six saucissons-ci sont six sous. Si ces six saucissons-ci sont six sous, ces six saucissons-ci sont trop chers.

Hello madame sausage-seller! How much are these six sausages? These six sausages are six cents. If these are six cents, these six sausages are too expensive.

Je veux et j'exige qu'un chasseur sachant chasser sans ses èchasses sache chasser sans son chien de chasse.

I want and demand that a hunter who knows how to hunt without his stilts knows how to hunt without his hunting dog.

Ce sont seize cent jacynthes sèches dans seize cent sachets secs.

There are 600 dry hyacinths in 600 dry sachets.

Ce sont trois très gros rats dans trois très gros trous roulant trois gros rats gris morts.

There are three fat rats in three fat rat-holes rolling three fat grey dead rats.

English tongue twisters

After your French friends have laughed at you, let them try these tongue twisters in English.

If neither he sells seashells, nor she sells seashells, who shall sell seashells? Shall seashells be sold?	Si ni lui ni elle ne vendent de coquillages, qui les vendra? Les coquillages seront-ils vendus?
Peter Piper picked a peck of pickled peppers.	Pierre Pipant a choisi un picotin de cornichons.
Rugged rubber baby buggy bumpers.	Des pare-chocs solides en caoutchoue pour les voitures d'enfants.
The sixth sick sheik's sixth sheep's sick.	Le sixième mouton du sixième sheik est malade.
Red bug's blood and black bug's blood.	Sang d'insecte rouge, sang d'insecte noir.
Soldiers' shoulders.	Epaules de soldats.
Thieves seize skis.	Les voleurs s'emparent de skis.
I'm a pleasant mother pheasant plucker. I pluck mother pheasants. I'm the most pleasant mother pheasant plucker that ever plucked a mother pheasant.	Je suis une plaisant plumeur de faisanes. Je plume les faisanes. Je suis le plumeur de faisanes le plus plaisant qui ait jamais plumé de faisanes.

French Gestures

Here are a few common French gestures and their meanings:

The Fingertips Kiss: Gently bring the fingers and thumb of your right hand together, raise to your lips, kiss lightly, and toss your fingers and thumb into the air. Be careful, tourists look silly when they over-emphasize this subtle action. It can mean sexy, delicious, divine, or wonderful.

The Eyelid Pull: Place your extended forefinger below the center of your eye, and pull the skin downward. This means: "I'm alert. I'm looking. You can't fool me."

The Roto-Wrist: Hold your forearm out from your waist with your open palm down, and pivot your wrist clockwise and counter-clockwise like you're opening a doorknob. When a Frenchman uses this gesture while explaining something to you, he isn't sure of the information—or it's complete B.S.

The Chin Flick: Tilt your head back slightly, and flick the back of your fingers forward in an arc from under your chin. This means: "I'm not interested."

To beckon someone: In northern Europe you bring your palm up, and in France and the south you wave it down. To Americans this looks like "go away"—not the invitation it really is.

Let's Talk Telephones

Smart travelers use the telephone every day to make hotel reservations, check on tourist information, or call home. The card-operated public phones are easier to use than coin-operated phones. Buy a *télécarte* (phone card) at a post office, tourist office, train station, or *tabac* (tobacco shop). The smallest value is between 40-50 francs (about $8). The price of a call, local or international, will automatically be deducted from your card as you use it. At the *télécarte* phone booths, follow the instructions that will prompt you to: (1) *decrochez*—pick up the receiver; (2) *insérez votre carte*—insert your card; (3) *patientez*—wait; and (4) *composez votre numero*—dial your number. France's newest phone card, called KOSMOS, is not inserted into a phone, but allows you to dial from the comfort of your hotel room (or anywhere). KOSMO calls costs less per minute than *télécarte* calls, but KOSMOS takes longer to use because you have to dial a lot of numbers (clear instructions in English on card).

European time is six/nine hours ahead of the east/west coast of the United States. Breakfast in Paris is midnight in California.

Dialing Direct

Calling Between Countries: Dial the international access code (00 for most European countries, 011 for America), the country code of the country you're calling, the area code (if it it starts with zero, drop the zero), and then the local number. See international access codes and country codes below.

Specifics on Calls Between France and the U.S.A: To call France from the U.S.A., dial our international access code (011), the French country code (33), drop the initial zero of the ten-digit number, then dial the rest of the number. To call the U.S.A. from France, dial 00-1-area code-local number.

Calling Long Distance Within Most European Countries (except France): First dial the area code (including its zero), then the local number.

Calling Long Distance Within France: France is unusual because it lacks area codes. If you're calling within France, dial the ten-digit telephone number whether you're calling across the country or across the street.

Europe's Exceptions: Most European countries do have area codes. These don't: France, Italy, Spain, Norway, and Denmark. For direct-dialing specifics on France, see above. To make an international call to Italy, Spain, Norway, or Denmark, dial the international access code (usually 00), the country code, and then the local number in its entirety. To make long-distance calls within any of these countries, simply dial the local number.

International Access Codes
When dialing direct, first dial the international access code of the country you're calling from. For most countries, it's "00." The few exceptions are Spain (07), Sweden (009), and the U.S.A./Canada (011).

Country Codes
After dialing the international access code, dial the code of the country you're calling.

Austria—43	France—33	Netherlands—31
Belgium—32	Germany—49	Norway—47
Britain—44	Greece—30	Portugal—351
Czech Rep.—420	Ireland—353	Spain—34
Denmark—45	Italy—39	Sweden—46
Estonia—372	Latvia—371	Switzerland—41
Finland—358	Lithuania—370	U.S.A./Canada—1

U.S.A. Direct Services: Calling Card Operators
It's cheaper to call direct, but if you have a calling card and prefer to have an English-speaking operator dial for you, here are the numbers: ATT (0800 - 990 - 011), MCI (0800 - 990 - 019), and SPRINT (0800 - 990 - 087).

Weather:
First line is average daily low (°F); second line average daily high (°F); third line, days of no rain.

	J	F	M	A	M	J	J	A	S	O	N	D
Paris	32	34	36	41	47	52	55	55	50	44	38	33
	42	45	52	60	67	73	76	75	69	59	49	43
	16	15	16	16	18	19	19	19	19	17	15	14
Riviera	40	41	45	49	56	62	66	66	62	55	48	43
	56	56	59	64	69	76	81	81	77	70	62	58
	23	20	23	23	23	25	29	26	24	22	23	23

APPENDIX

Metric conversions (approximate):

1 inch = 25 millimeters	1 foot = .3 meter
1 yard = .9 meter	1 mile = 1.6 kilometers
1 sq. yard = .8 sq. meter	1 acre = 0.4 hectare
1 quart = .95 liter	1 ounce = 28 grams
1 pound = .45 kilo	1 kilo = 2.2 pounds
1 centimeter = 0.4 inch	1 meter = 39.4 inches

1 kilometer = .62 mile
Miles = kilometers divided by 2 plus 10%
(120 km ÷ 2 = 60, 60 +12 = 72 miles)
Fahrenheit degrees = double Celsius + 30

32° F = 0° C, 82° F = about 28° C

Your tear-out cheat sheet

Good day.	Bonjour.	bohn-zhoor
Do you speak English?	Parlez-vous anglais?	par-lay-voo ahn-glay
Yes. / No.	Oui. / Non.	wee / nohn
I don't speak French.	Je ne parle pas français.	zhuh nuh parl pah frahn-say
I'm sorry.	Désolé.	day-zoh-lay
Please.	S'il vous plaît.	see voo play
Thank you.	Merci.	mehr-see
No problem.	Pas de problème.	pah duh proh-blehm
It's good.	C'est bon.	say bohn
You are very kind.	Vous êtes très gentil.	vooz eht treh zhahn-tee
Goodbye.	Au revoir.	oh vwahr
Where is...?	Où est...?	oo ay
...a hotel	...un hôtel	uhn oh-tehl
...a youth hostel	...une auberge de jeunesse	ewn oh-behrzh duh zhuh-nehs
...a restaurant	...un restaurant	uhn rehs-toh-rahn
...a grocery store	...une épicerie	ewn ay-pee-suh-ree
...a pharmacy	...une pharmacie	ewn far-mah-see
...a bank	...une banque	ewn bahnk
...the train station	...la gare	lah gar
...the tourist info office	...l'office du tourisme	loh-fees dew too-reez-muh
Where are the toilets?	Où sont les toilettes?	oo sohn lay twah-leht
men / women	hommes / dames	ohm / dahm
How much is it?	Combien?	kohn-bee-an
Write it?	Ecrivez?	ay-kree-vay

Cheap.	Bon marché.	bohn mar-shay
Cheaper.	Moins cher.	mwan shehr
Cheapest.	Le moins cher.	luh mwan shehr
Is it free?	C'est gratuit?	say grah-twee
Included?	Inclus?	an-klew
Do you have...?	Avez-vous...?	ah-vay-voo
I would like...	Je voudrais...	zhuh voo-dray
We would like...	Nous voudrions...	noo voo-dree-ohn
...this.	...ceci.	suh-see
...just a little.	...un petit peu.	uhn puh-tee puh
...more.	...encore.	ahn-kor
...a ticket.	...un billet.	uhn bee-yay
...a room.	...une chambre.	ewn shahn-bruh
...the bill.	...l'addition.	lah-dee-see-ohn
one	un	uhn
two	deux	duh
three	trois	twah
four	quatre	kah-truh
five	cinq	sank
six	six	sees
seven	sept	seht
eight	huit	weet
nine	neuf	nuhf
ten	dix	dees
At what time?	À quelle heure?	ah kehl ur
Just a moment.	Un moment.	uhn moh-mahn
Now.	Maintenant.	man-tuh-nahn
soon / later	bientôt / plus tard	bee-an-toh / plew tar
today / tomorrow	aujourd'hui / demain	oh-zhoor-dwee / duh-man

Faxing your hotel reservation

Most hotel managers know basic "hotel English." Photocopy and enlarge this form, then fax away.

. . . .

One page fax   My fax #:_____

To: Today's date: ____ / ____ / ____
From: day month year

Dear Hotel _____,
    Please make this reservation for me:

Name: _____

Total # of people: ____ # of rooms: ____ # of nights: ____

Arriving: ____ / ____ / ____   Time of arrival (24-hour clock): _____
              day month year   (I will telephone if later)

Departing: ____ / ____ / ____
              day month year

Room(s): Single Double Twin   Triple Quad Quint
With: Toilet Shower   Bathtub   Sink only
Special needs: View   Quiet   Cheapest room   Ground floor

Credit card: Visa   Mastercard   American Express

Card #: _____   Exp. date: _____

Name on card: _____

If a deposit is necessary, you may charge me for the first night. Please fax or mail me confirmation of my reservation, along with the type of room reserved, the price, and whether the price includes breakfast. Thank you.

Signature: _____
Name: _____
Address :_____
Phone: _____   E-mail: _____

Rick Steves' Europe Through the Back Door Catalog

All of these items have been especially designed for independent budget travelers. They have been thoroughly field tested by Rick Steves and his globe-trotting ETBD staff, and are completely guaranteed. Prices include a free subscription to Rick's quarterly travel newsletter.

Back Door Bag convertible suitcase/backpack $75

At 9"x21"x13" this specially-designed, sturdy, functional bag is maximum carry-on-the-plane size (fits under the seat), and your key to foot-loose and fancy-free travel. Made in the USA from rugged, water-resistant 1000 denier Cordura nylon, it converts from a smart-looking suitcase to a handy backpack. It has hide-away padded shoulder straps, top and side handles, and a detachable shoulder strap (for toting as a suitcase). Beefy, lockable perimeter zippers allow easy access to the roomy (2500 cubic inches) main compartment. Two large outside pockets are perfect for frequently used items. A nylon stuff bag is also included. Over 50,000 Back Door travelers have used these bags around the world. Rick Steves helped design this bag, and lives out of it for 3 months at a time. Comparable bags cost much more. Available in black, navy blue and très chic forest green.

European railpasses

...cost the same everywhere, but only ETBD gives you a free hour-long "How to get the most out of your railpass" video, free advice on your itinerary, and your choice of one of Rick Steves' 13 country guidebooks or phrase books. For starters, call 425/771-8303, and we'll send you a free copy of Rick Steves' Annual Guide to European Railpasses.

Moneybelt $8

Absolutely required no matter where you're traveling! An ultra-light, sturdy, under-the-pants, one-size-fits-all nylon pouch, our svelte moneybelt is just the right size to carry your passport, airline tickets and traveler's checks comfortably. Made to ETBD's exacting specifications, this moneybelt is your best defense against theft—when you wear it, feeling a street urchin's hand in your pocket becomes just another interesting cultural experience.

Prices are good through 2000—maybe longer. Orders will be processed within 2 weeks. Call us at (425) 771-8303 or go to www.ricksteves.com for details on shipping/handling charges and local sales tax. Send your check to:

Rick Steves' Europe Through the Back Door

130 Fourth Ave. N, PO Box 2009
Edmonds, WA 98020

www.ricksteves.com

More books by Rick Steves...

Now more than ever, travelers are determined to get the most out of every mile, minute and dollar. That's what Rick's books are all about. He'll help you have a better trip because you're on a budget, not in spite of it. Each of these books is published by John Muir Publications, and is available through your local bookstore, or through Rick's free travel newsletter.

Rick Steves' France, Belgium & the Netherlands
Rick Steves' Paris

For a successful trip, raw information isn't enough. In his country and city guidebooks, Rick weeds through each region's endless possibilities to give you candid, straight-forward advice on what to see, where to sleep, how to manage your time, and how to get the most out of every dollar. Besides France and Paris, the series includes....

Rick Steves' Best of Europe
Rick Steves' Italy
Rick Steves' Germany, Austria & Switzerland
(with Prague)
Rick Steves' Great Britain & Ireland
Rick Steves' London
Rick Steves' Scandinavia
Rick Steves' Spain & Portugal
Rick Steves' Russia & the Baltics

Rick Steves' Europe Through The Back Door

Updated every year, *ETBD* has given thousands of people the skills and confidence they needed to travel through the less-touristed "back doors" of Europe. You'll find chapters on packing, itinerary-planning, transportation, finding rooms, travel photography, keeping safe and healthy, plus chapters on Rick's favorite back door discoveries.

Mona Winks: Self-Guided Tours of Europe's Top Museums

Let's face it, museums can ruin a good vacation. But *Mona* takes you by the hand, giving you fun and easy-to-follow self-guided tours through Europe's 20 most frightening and exhausting museums and cultural obligations. Packed with more than 200 maps and illustrations.

Europe 101: History and Art for the Traveler

A lively, entertaining crash course in European history and art, *Europe 101* is the perfect way to prepare yourself for the rich cultural smorgasbord that awaits you.

Rick Steves' Postcards from Europe

For twenty-five years Rick Steves has been exploring Europe, sharing his tricks and discoveries in guidebooks and on TV. Now, in *Postcards from Europe* he shares his favorite personal travel stories and his off-beat European friends – all told in that funny, down-to-earth style that makes Rick his Mom's favorite guidebook writer.

Rick Steves' European Phrase Books: French, Italian, German, Spanish/Portuguese, and French/Italian/German

Finally, a series of phrase books written especially for the budget traveler! Each book gives you the words and phrases you need to communicate with the locals about room-finding, food, health and transportation—all spiced with Rick Steves' travel tips, and his unique blend of down-to-earth practicality and humor.

What we do at Europe Through the Back Door

At ETBD we value travel as a powerful way to better understand and contribute to the world in which we live. Our mission at ETBD is to equip travelers with the confidence and skills necessary to travel through Europe independently, economically, and in a way that is culturally broadening. To accomplish this, we:

■ Teach budget European travel skills seminars;

■ Research and write guidebooks to Europe;

■ Write and host a public television series;

■ Sell European railpasses, our favorite guidebooks, travel videos, bags, and accessories;

■ Provide European travel consulting services;

■ Organize and lead free-spirited no-grumps small-group Back Door tours of Europe;

■ Sponsor our European Travel Resource Center near Seattle, and our Web site at www.ricksteves.com

...and we travel a lot.

Back Door 'Best of Europe' tours

If you like our independent travel philosophy but would like to benefit from the camaraderie and efficiency of group travel, our Back Door tours may be right up your alley. Every year we lead friendly, intimate 'Best of Europe' tours, free-spirited 'Bus, Bed & Breakfast' tours, and regional tours of France, Italy, Britain, Ireland, Germany-Austria-Switzerland, Spain-Portugal, Scandinavia, and Turkey. For details, call 425/771-8303 or go to www.ricksteves.com and ask for our free tour booklet.